Shaking Hands with Love

Shaking Hands with *Love*

Our Ongoing Journey

A True Story of Telepathic Communication with Spirit Guides

Gina Ravenswood

Cover design by Lance Ravenswood

Some names have been changed to protect identity.

Balboa Press books may be ordered through booksellers or by contacting:

Balboa Press
A Division of Hay House
1663 Liberty Drive
Bloomington, IN 47403
www.balboapress.com.au
1-(877) 407-4847

ISBN: 978-1-4525-0881-8 (sc)
ISBN: 978-1-4525-0882-5 (e)

Printed in the United States of America

Balboa Press rev. date: 1/24/2013

To my eldest children, Grant, Adrian, and Anmea;
and my two youngest, Lance, and Celeste, whose
youthful energy helped me keep my feet on the ground
throughout my times of inspiration for this book.

"Love is only love when it is moving".
Lalesha

Contents

Preface

Gina Ravenswood, a New Zealand medium, tells the true story of her friend Nannette's battle with cancer. Their friendship withstood not only the test of time in this world but spanned the afterlife as well. The first part of the book is about Nannette getting cancer and her transition from her earth life, and this is followed by her experiences on the Other Side. The second part of the book is filled with colourful conversations between Gina, Nannette, and spirit guides as they help the author clarify her own personal experiences with love.

This is their story, which opens up another dimension of love.

Chapter 1

The Right Door

I stepped briskly up the stairs of the Rotorua Hospital. My dearest friend, Nannette, was in ward eight recovering from an operation for stomach pains. Why take the lift? After a night of drifting between sleep, meditation, and prayer, I was on a high, fully positive from my interaction with spirit. *This spiritual friend of mine will recover,* I thought, the phrase resounding through my mind. My legs felt energised; I wanted to take two steps at a time.

"Don't walk so fast, Mummy," said my four-year-old son, Lance, clutching at my hand.

Before I could answer, we were both forced to stop still. On the next level, we were confronted by a huge sign over the door: Ward Closed, Alterations in Progress.

"Take the lift, Mummy; it will lead us the right way."

I smiled because even a child knows instinctively there is always a right way and a wrong way to walk the road of life. Quite often I was shown guidance in the form of roads, hills, and especially steps; they were symbolic of our ongoing journey.

Entering the lift, I wondered why I was so enthusiastic when I woke up that morning. Was it a sign that Nannette would survive? By the time we turned the corner into ward eight, the high in my mind had gone, and doubt had started to surface. A cold shudder moved through me; at the same time, I could feel sadness welling up in my heart. In the past few years, three of my closest friends had departed from life. Was this another friend who would die? Growing up in a large family with older parents, I had experienced many aunts and uncles passing on; because I had been a child, they had seemed old, so it was easier to accept their departure. Nannette was a spiritual friend; her helpful dedication to my work as a medium and writer was in progress. I knew change brought inevitable movement, but this would be a big change for many people, including myself.

I tried hard to put aside my own feelings as we entered the right door. Finding Nannette, I sat on her bed and bent over to give her a kiss; her breath was bitter. I could smell the cancer; my underlying fears were confirmed. She was still sedated after the operation, so I settled into a chair, contemplating how I was going to help her through this predicament. I saw a door to the Other Side arrive beside her; an angelic presence appeared above her. I had seen this before when another friend was ready to depart their earthly life.

Lance climbed onto my knee, cuddling up to go to sleep. He was tired, so I decided to return home to get him into bed. I also wanted to sort out my feelings of personal attachment with her as a friend and her own personal journey with her soul, which was really more important at this time than me missing her. She had a loving husband; his grief would be greater. I was a medium; therefore, with my knowledge of the Other Side, I should be able to let her go more easily.

Letting go with unconditional love is something that we all have to exercise at different stages in our life, and it's always difficult. More knowledge about the Other Side does make this easier.

Drawing on the energy I had started the day with, I took Lance's hand, and we walked into the car park. I couldn't help noticing how clear the night was—it was the middle of winter, yet the stars were shining like a summer's evening. I took a huge breath, focusing on one bright star that jumped out at me. I will never forget that moment: the star seemed to move closer, reflecting energy to me, and as the light glided through me, I felt tall and expanded. I knew that feeling—the presence of spirit could not be denied. Tears welled up in my eyes, falling down my face like a soothing balm. My heart seemed to be unravelling through time, joining love and pain with the silent acceptance of our ongoing journey. Lance also had tears in his eyes.

"Mummy, I don't think I will see Nannette again."

"No, darling, she may become a star like that one."

"Then she will see me!"

Confidently I answered, "Yes, she will."

As I turned the key in my old car, the noise of the engine jolted me back to the reality that I had to drive a long way home that night, yet my experience with the star had reality too. These two states of awareness became part of my life over the next few months. I quickly moved from grief to acceptance because Nannette was about to face the biggest challenge in her life. My belief and understanding of her situation had to be clear and without too much emotion, or else it would interfere—and I'd become too drained and unable to help. The drive home went smoothly. Lance was so good, falling asleep as soon as the car started. My energy was strong; maybe spirit had given me an extra dose this morning to help me cope with what was to be. I thought it indicated that she would survive, but after today's experience, I knew that another door was opening for Nannette. I had to be there for her.

As a medium, I have found that when a person is ready to depart their earth life, the energy surrounding this process can be exhilarating for some—and incredibly sad for others. I have analysed this and found the ones that depart with positive energy have usually fulfilled their lives, and those that depart with sadness are unfulfilled. I have also concluded that it doesn't really matter what one dies of; it's fulfilling one's soul blueprint while alive that is so important. Living each day to the fullest is vital; what we do, whom we love, and how we think all contribute to our next destinations.

Chapter 2

Friendship

Nannette had been a true friend, helping me with my difficult second marriage and always going out of her way to encourage my work as a medium. She admired how, at any given time, I could raise my energy to a higher level, thereby gaining insight and understanding from higher beings known as spirit guides. I am sure this came about because, as I was growing up, my parents didn't indoctrinate my mind with any religious beliefs. They didn't even question the things I would say about the future, even when they came true. I had freedom, and I was accepted. Therefore, I could indulge my mind in thinking about what I could see, feel, and hear. I could always feel the presence of spirit, often having positive dreams that eventuated. This gave me a desire to understand the unseen; I wanted to work it out for myself, and I was left alone to do this.

My humble parents gave my two sisters, my brother, and me the wonderful opportunity to grow up with an uncluttered mind, which is maybe why we were all interested in the unseen. The visions I had gave me a yearning to know and understand the reason behind what happened in life. As

I searched in the early '70s, investigating many spiritual beliefs, my first husband and I were privileged enough to meet a very ordinary, humble man who channelled a spirit guide. He lived in a small flat surrounded by trees at the end of an avenue in the city of Tauranga, New Zealand. He became my mentor, and we would visit him every Friday night. The evenings consisted of lots of cups of tea, listening to music, and discussing the future of this planet, and then he would turn on a tape recorder, take a deep breath, and speak. It was amazing—the words from his spirit guide flowed with understandings that clarified the suffering states we all find ourselves in.

It didn't take long before my mind had raised itself to the level where I could channel a spirit guide. From then on, every time I yearned for an answer, a message would flow back from a spirit guide. The higher I aspired, the deeper the message would be. I found that I could stretch my mind into other dimensions easily and still feel connected to my earthly self. In fact, the higher I expanded my mind, the happier I felt with my earthly life. I could remain within this feeling of higher consciousness for hours.

Viewing the people I knew from this compassionate centre would make all my friends look loving, even if, on this human plane, they had a conflict with me. If I held my concentration, one of my friends would occasionally communicate telepathically with me over any disagreement. Sometimes the relayed words were as wise as the spirit guides I had come to know. When I discovered that everybody has a soul connected to his or her physical self, it all made sense. This is the part of God we are all connected to as a family, and it never dies.

Gradually, the soul became more real and more important to me than the garment—the physical self. I was a mother of three children at the time and discovered that, when I looked into their eyes, if I acknowledged that they had souls, they instantly responded. This made it easier to relate to them, as loving children on this higher level would immediately put them into a state of 'wanting to please'. Higher levels of energy became my greatest interest; sometimes this would take precedence and chaos would rule the day. Amongst this blur of activity, I constantly sought the spirit guides' advice, finding their clarity invaluable to my human life.

Nannette had experienced a lot of wisdom from my spirit guides; she had incorporated this with her own ability as a nurse and then later as a counsellor. She wished to share this understanding with others, putting effort into organising groups where people could be exposed to higher viewpoints. Her plan was already in motion, and I was part of it, yet I knew her illness meant my cycle with her was about to end. My mind rolled over our friendship—something was incomplete.

Moving into higher energy, I questioned this. A spirit guide relayed these words to me: "Your purpose with Nannette has only just begun. What you will experience, you will forget. However, it will remain with you as a light. Years will pass, time for your human self to catch up to your destiny, then you will remember. There are lessons you need to live through before your link with Nannette can express. Your memory will be a wonderful friend to you in the future."

Although I couldn't quite foresee what the spirit guide meant, that night, the words enabled me to drift into a very deep sleep. The next day, I started to catch up on housework. As I was vacuuming, the friend who had taught me to channel appeared in my lounge with a smile on his face. For a moment, I forgot he was on the Other Side and went to ask him to move out of the way of the vacuum cleaner. Embarrassed, I sat down. He didn't speak, but his smile changed to a grin. As I remembered my love for him, I reminded myself he still existed on another dimension, and communication was always possible.

He would know what the future held for Nannette; even though he didn't relay this information to me, his smile was enough to let me know the whole situation was guided. It is amazing how when we are reassured that something in our lives is meant to be, we get the energy to go through it.

The vacuum cleaning had to wait as I meditated on the love and knowledge that reside on other dimensions that are only a thought away.

Chapter 3

Nannette's Wish

My mornings always consisted of a walk before breakfast. If I woke up early enough, I would see the sun coming up across the water by the small harbour in New Zealand where I lived. The newness of another day seen with the contrasting colours of early morning was inspiring.

Walking on the flat grass by the sand and sea would unravel any anxieties I was retaining. This path led to the point of a peninsular, continuing up a hill through the Omokoroa Reserve filled with one-hundred-year-old trees planted by early settlers. Then it would even out onto a flat pathway once more, where you could view the mountain ranges in the distance, abundantly covered in native bush. This impressive walk would prepare my body and mind for the day ahead. Three days had passed since I had seen Nannette, and I would visit her today. The hospital was an hour and a half away, an opportune amount of time to contemplate my purpose with her.

Calmness surrounded me as I entered the hospital. The scene was happy; Nannette's much-loved husband, Mike, looked relieved. I waited for family to go and then seated myself close by Nannette.

"Are you in any pain?" I asked.

"No, dear, none. And the operation went well. The surgeon visited me this morning; he did his best to remove all the cancer. I am hopeful since he is a good surgeon. I used to work with him in theatre years ago while nursing. We had a good talk. I'm a little tired, but I'm preparing myself for the recovery time. This is what I wish to speak to you about. When I return home in a few days, friends have offered to assist me through this healing process. I would like to ask your spirit guide's advice. My wish is—if I recover with spiritual help—I can give proof to others." With an appealing smile, she asked, "What do you think?"

When confronted by such a positive request, my immediate reaction was to say yes. However, I remembered what a spirit guide had said to me in previous years: "Those that search for proof will miss the truth contained within."

I couldn't answer her. A cool breeze from spirit entered the room, followed by stillness. I looked at Nannette, and she put her head down. Silent moments passed. Raising her head, eyes directly focused at me, almost threateningly, she asked again, "Don't you think it would be a good idea?"

"Yes." As I surrendered to her plea, I felt disconnected from everything in the room—even Nannette. I found myself swimming in a pulsating energy that was lifting me high above my human self; angelic presences were present. I knew her wish wasn't meant to be, but I courageously pretended her idea was right. The energy in the room stayed very still and cold, but safe; spirit wasn't backing her wish.

"Can you please pass me the blanket, dear? I'm a little cold," Nannette said. "I think I will sleep now."

Bending over, I placed the hospital blanket over Nannette. Her body looked so small. I waited until she fell asleep, and then I quietly departed.

Driving home, I found myself yearning for a sunny day and a warm climate; the coldness of this situation, coupled with winter's chill, was affecting me. Nannette had many friends who were natural health practitioners; these loved ones were preparing to assist her through the fight to overcome any remaining cancer. As one of her closest friends, I was to play a part in her recovery. *Maybe I have it wrong—maybe the spirit guides with all their light will prevent Nannette's body from dying.*

I received this message from a spirit guide: "You cannot turn the clock back, and who is to say dying is dead matter?"

These words reminded me of our eternal journey. Reflecting on the insights I had experienced with others that had passed over, I remembered they were far from being morbid or sad. Most souls on the Other Side were happy to be there; it was the ones left behind who suffered.

I started to accept it was Nannette's time to continue her journey in the afterlife. This cheered me up, yet by the time I arrived home, I was confused again. Even the loving embraces from my two youngest children couldn't clear it from me. I decided to go to bed early with the thought: *Spirit, help me accept the true outcome.*

I slept soundly, only to be awakened in the night by Nannette. I sat up in bed, eyes open, staring at her glowing form.

"Nannette, have you died?"

"No, dear, but I will."

I could not ignore the love she emanated as these words telepathically resounded toward my mind. Then, in a haze of gold light, she departed. I drifted into a deep sleep, saying to myself, "I will remember this. I will remember."

The next day was different; the calm presence from Nannette's visitation was with me, giving strength and detachment. Acceptance had entered my emotions and made them feel like a still, calm bay where everything melts into one. I acknowledged my dream was real, and I knew I must follow this guidance and help her prepare for her transition to the Other Side.

Chapter 4

The Transition Begins

I had promised Nannette I would visit her every week. Since I lived so far away, the whole day was needed if I was going to spend quality time with her. As I drove to Rotorua that Friday, it seemed to take one and a half days instead of one and a half hours.

My mind was living through something else—separate from the loving friends and family's kind help for her recovery. Part of me was working on another level toward Nannette's transition from her earthly life. I was aware of this because the previous night's visitation had left an imprint on my clairvoyant mind; it had also contained love and happiness, reassuring me it was her destiny. I could not forget her glowing form; compared to her frail physical body, it was far more alive.

I concentrated on my driving. It was a cold, damp winter's day. A storm had left debris over parts of the road, and many trees had been pulled out by the roots. As I waited in the traffic for trucks to remove the blockage, I remembered a poem I once wrote:

Broken down tree, you are the windswept version of life
I can tell the summer sun has scorched you dry
Autumn has revealed you to the harshness of winter's cold
Soon spring will come and renew you with yet another fever
And you will not grow old until another cycle takes its toll
Broken down tree, you resemble me
We need the sun, the warmth and care,
Wind and rain to change and clear
The cold, the still, hours to kill
Rebirth, release concealed beneath
Fashioned in cycles for all to see live the seasons of time.

Startled by the sound of horns, I moved the car into gear, driving off through the now-cleared road.

Entering Nannette's home was like a spring day; friends had been cleaning the house, and soup was simmering on the stove. Music echoed throughout the rooms. The eyes of loved ones were filled with hope. Nannette was sitting up in bed, smiling. I felt like the Grim Reaper. In the serenity of Nannette's room, I sat within two opposing energies—living and dying.

"Thank you for coming, dear," said Nannette. "I'm ready for you to channel to me. What I really want to know is why I got cancer after years of good diet and disciplining myself to follow a spiritual pathway. I would like to know what I have done wrong. Is it my karma? Am I being punished? It is my right to know why."

I had never heard Nannette be so demanding; normally I would feel nervous, but the spirit guide had definitely prepared me. Strength coursed through my nervous system. I also wanted to know why! I knew every case was individual through my work as a medium—this had given me understanding over the many different reasons a person departs earth life—but I did find it difficult with Nannette because she was beginning a new cycle with me. She had worked so hard toward it that the thought of her dying didn't make sense.

I turned on my recording devise, prepared to channel. Before the spirit guide started to speak through me, I looked at Nannette. Another dimension opened up. Her face was fading; as it did, other faces started to appear, differing in colour and nationality. Each face would recede at a certain age; the essence of Nannette looked at me through each changing face. The room was swimming in light; Nannette bowed her head as if the light was hurting her eyes.

"What is happening to me, dear? I feel I am trapped in a time zone."

Clearly and slowly, the spirit guide explained to Nannette that she was revisiting her past lives on another level. Even though she couldn't see the faces of who she had been, she would feel her past experiences. Unconsciously she had been reviewing these past lives. Nannette believed in reincarnation, so what the spirit guide was saying made sense to her.

"Am I paying off past debts now?" she bravely asked the spirit guide.

"The trauma you are going through now does have its origin in a previous life. Who, where, and when doesn't matter as it all ends up as energy, but how this can occur is important to understand. All people are born with a heart—the doorway to the soul; and a mind—the seat of consciousness or belief. When a person's mind believes something that is out of tune with their heart or contrary to their feelings, imbalance begins. This friction creates negative energy, and if this energy is not corrected, it follows them to the Other Side where it is held until a future life when it can be cleared.

"There was one life where you were obsessed with power and perfection. You turned your back on your heart; your true loving self became imprisoned during this time. It was not that great emphasis was placed on wrongdoing; balance had to be attained to set you free. You entered other lifetimes where you expressed from your heart and much was worked through. However, the remaining imbalance came with you into this lifetime in the form of energy. This energy has been your own personal suffering; it is the unfulfilment deep within you. You have always felt this and have tried hard to correct it by living a spiritual life. The human you has played its part well, and now your soul has made the extreme choice of ending your earthly cycle. This is your time of release; as you contemplate your life, you will learn soul has the final say. Your soul overlooks you as you try to realise its choice."

"I can feel it now," Nannette uttered to my guide. "I want to get better to help others, but my body won't respond. It feels separate to me."

"Your heart and your mind are still going in different directions," the spirit guide gently explained. "One can throw oneself out of balance by wanting what is not one's destiny. This creates karma, yet one can become free from this restriction by listening to the heart (the doorway to the soul). You are trying to create a destiny—when your soul has already made its decision. Your dream was to enlighten others; it still is. Spirit hears your call—you feel the desire—yet you cannot see the plan. Your suffering is from your mind as it remains set upon organising the way people can be enlightened. You are limited by this mindset—and by putting all your eggs in one basket called this one physical life. As you think in this way, you confine your soul. You sentence yourself to a time, thereby creating limitations your soul is not happy with. The unhappiness inside of you has been present for a long time. Not one person you love is to blame for this confinement. When they love you, you are not there. Your love is elsewhere. Love is preparing you for your final journey. Take comfort that all your dreams will eventually come true."

A loud knock on the door abruptly brought me out of trance. Mike entered, "Another friend to see you love, she wants to know if you would like some healing?"

"Yes," said Nannette. "Show them in."

She turned to me and said, "Thank you for that, dear. I will listen to the recording. Can you stay for dinner?"

I stayed and observed; what I saw was interesting. While the healer was giving light and love through their hands onto Nanette's stomach, I witnessed about twenty other pairs of white hands from spirit, pouring light onto her head. Nannette was merging with these hands of light from above; her mind was absorbing higher consciousness. The relief showed on her face.

The healer felt the cancer was moving; in my mind, Nannette was moving closer to the Other Side by giving over to the light above her. I believe this unseen activity prevented Nannette from feeling pain. It was a mystery to the medical doctors why, from the time of the operation until six months later when her body died, no drugs were used because she suffered no pain; this was a real phenomenon.

My understanding is that—with a combination of healing from good people and love from spirit—Nannette's earthly vibration was raised enough to connect with her soul; this gave her a constant flow of energy from spirit, thereby enabling natural morphine, endorphins, to release themselves.

As I drove home, the cold, damp night didn't worry me. I was too busy thinking about soul destiny and what a relief it was to accept it. Even though I knew I would have to go through things I would rather not go through, I was ready to listen to my soul. If it has the final say, why waste time procrastinating. My marriage was in a state of disarray because I had ignored those intuitive feelings we all have. I kept on going, wanting everything to come right.

As I made my decision to accept my true pathway, warmth flowed through me, and acceptance felt like the first step on a pathway toward reality. The reality I wanted was to work with what was going to eventuate, rather than creating a separate pathway. This whole experience was helping me. What was the point in focusing toward a future that would never be? Some say 'live in the moment', yet when you include soul, the present contains fragments of the past and the future. If we knew what truly lay ahead, we'd work with it—not against it. Knowing Nannette's soul destiny was to pass over gave me the strength to remain on the thread of love for her departure rather than opposing her soul by trying to help her live.

Arriving home, I could see my marriage would not last. How or when this would happen didn't bother me anymore. I just knew that, because of acceptance, my life was shifting into a pathway I couldn't see at that stage. I could feel its peace, and this gave me enough strength to withstand the opposition from my husband, who was fanatically against my work. I also learned that to accept opposition without retaliating was to remove the fight; arguments cannot be fuelled without a fight. Peace slept beside me that night.

Chapter 5

A Short Recovery

For a few weeks, Nannette didn't need me to go over, and I remained at home. Since I knew she would have to process what the spirit guide had said, I left her alone. Alterations were in progress at my house and my three- and four-year-olds needed constant supervision. My marriage was showing sure signs of dissolving; my husband was going off on tangents and spending the money set aside for the extension. The builder, plumber, and electrician all looked nervous about being paid; tension filled the air. The adjustments to the home were coming into clear perspective, not the inhabitants—or maybe we were! Looking back, going in different directions was guided, even then. Without considering and accepting there was a greater plan, I could not have made it through that time. I felt the entire financial load on my shoulders—and it came to pass. Every day I would do what was necessary for the day. Remaining with guidance was my stability.

Phone conversations with Nannette sounded surprisingly clear; as always, she would ask me about my marriage. She reminded me they were there for me any time I chose to leave, and although it was difficult to balance my energy between my failing marriage and Nanette's illness, I knew it was not the right time to leave. Nannette was convinced she was recovering, and our original ability to converse on a higher level was returning. This didn't faze me; I knew it was part of her learning to go through this process. Occasionally, I would doubt my guidance, but every time this happened, a sign would appear.

A sign appeared one morning when Nannette and Mike arrived on my doorstep. Nannette was looking great; she explained how the natural medicine had started to work. Mike was smiling, happy to have his soul mate back. As I observed this joy, I let go of what I knew, joining them in discussions about the future. We all sat down to share lunch on our laps since the furniture had been moved to enable the builders to work.

"Don't the alterations look great," said Nannette. "You will be happy to have the extra room at long last; the children will have more freedom."

"Well, changes should bring freedom," I replied. "Life should be about movement. Our souls are always moving; it is only our human self that lags behind."

At the same moment I spoke these words, I caught Nannette's eyes. She immediately looked away into the distance. The same cool breeze present at the hospital entered the room, but this time Mike put his head down. It started raining and silent moments passed, making the house feel very cold.

"We had better start the drive home," said Nannette. "Will you come over on Friday, dear? The group would love to see you."

"Yes," I replied. As they drove off, I centred myself back into my own guidance. The reality of the situation or what was going to happen in the future wasn't present with that visit. I started yearning for the comfort and warmth of physical love since my husband and I were already sleeping in different rooms. I realised that this is how Nannette must feel; she didn't want to lose the warmth of human love and let go of her life as Nannette. This I had no answer for.

After much contemplation, I decided to drive over on Friday to share in the temporary recovery Nannette was making. However, by the time I arrived, a backward step had been taken—she was back in bed. The family looked disappointed, nervous. Returning to my original role, I sat down by Nannette. She once again asked my spirit guide what was happening.

The guide was very direct. "Dear one, you are fifty per cent wanting to live, and fifty per cent wanting to die. As this battle goes on within you, your physical body takes the strain. When cells oppose each other, disease flourishes."

These words had an effect; Nannette went into a deep sleep. I was awakened out of my trance by her snoring; she looked peaceful. I could feel her soul's presence; it was so loving and kind. How sad that her heart and mind, by not being in harmony, had created this situation; now it was too late to reverse the effects. From what I have witnessed, the energy from our hearts needs to be expressed in our living—and so does the energy from our minds. Knowing this has made me more determined to fulfil my own life. From that time on, I have treated my body like a vehicle for my heart and mind. Every day I check the energy I wake up with and make sure I can feel energy from both. I then express it, hoping that by the time I depart this lifetime, I am emptied out and ready for the next world of expression that lies ahead for each of us.

Driving home that evening, I wondered whether Nannette was taking her time to depart because she knew loved ones would miss her; perhaps she was giving them time to adjust. I knew every person involved was being touched by the presence of spirit; I could feel it overlooking the whole scene. I came to the conclusion that it was what it was.

"No!" a spirit guide telepathically echoed to me.

So much for having my own thoughts! I slowed down to listen on a quiet stretch of road.

The spirit guide continued, "This does happen. A lot of souls frequently delay their passing to allow their loved ones time to adjust, but not with Nannette. She is still attached to her earth life from fear of the unknown. Until this fear is processed and removed, she will not let go. As she moves in and out of consciousness, it will naturally happen. Be there when she does let go; she will need you."

In my life, if I was ever asked to help, energy would always come to me. I could not work out when I would be needed, but these words made me realise it wasn't far off. Arriving home, I could feel a distinct ending to my trips to Rotorua. My three-year-cycle with Nannette was about to end. I could do nothing but wait for her time of letting go.

Chapter 6

Letting Go

Once again, Friday became the regular time to visit Nannette. If my spirit guide was asked for a message, the same words were repeated: *You are fifty per cent wanting to live, fifty per cent wanting to die.*

Thereby acknowledging to Nannette, what was hers: her own will that was still holding on. A range of emotions could be seen in the concerned eyes and helpful hands of friends and family. At times, I felt like an intruder, wishing I could turn the clock back to happier days in her home. I couldn't; nobody could. We were all powerless at this stage.

These weekly visits were becoming an ordeal. To keep myself positive, I would sit in a cafe by Lake Rotorua, drinking coffee and meditating until I could feel some energy. Then I would drive to her home. Sometimes I would channel; other times, I couldn't speak, but my eyes locked into her eyes. I knew communication was happening on another level.

This particular Friday was different. As I drank my coffee, I could not generate any energy to visit her. The waiter kept asking if I was okay. Unable to break out of my trance, I started writing. I informed the waiter about my friend, and he left me alone.

As soon as I put pen to paper, I realised it was time to let go. I looked across at the lake; it radiated a deep blue. I started to dream-off, thinking about the lake weed that had polluted this vast beautiful lake; experts were working on a system to purify the water. I thought of Nannette's cancer; it was like a weed. The ugliness of this world was pulling me down to a level of despondency—until my spirit guide arrived. I started to write the words down:

> *Love is a multitude of fragmented thoughts and feelings. All people have a soul, and because the soul won't allow itself to be polluted, it stands back, only flowing when it can resonate with love. Love has become impure in your world; this is why soul finds it hard to express. When you begin life as a child, you naturally reach to connect with love; rarely does it flow, for most people have been hurt over love; therefore, not many parents can freely function from their soul centre.*
>
> *Examine the centres you come from; if love is not flowing, then your soul won't be present. Love has a stabilising effect on life. When one makes a soul decision, love is released; this includes letting go. Pain and suffering are the result of separation; this is why letting go is difficult, for inside all people is an innate desire to join together. This comes from the soul's natural yearning to reunite. Love has the ingredient to make this happen.*

> *The universe cannot function without love—so how can you? Follow love and fulfil its purpose, and when you find there is no love in your personal world, know the process of letting go is still working. When the process is complete, love will be there for you. There are no broken dreams, only different realities.*
>
> *Gaps are created by the human mind, for it takes time to work situations out. Analysing never gives you a true understanding of your life; your love does because the way you work out your life is not the real you—your love is.*
>
> *Take comfort in the truth that when Nannette leaves her earthly life, she will be embraced by love. Understand the time she is taking to move forward is governed by the remaining fear she has; she is at the stage where she is questioning what she did right, and where she went wrong. As her mind reflects on her life, she processes the last pieces. This can be done whilst she is unconscious, and when it is all processed, she will depart this life. She shall visit you at a future time.*

Somewhere in the spirit guide's message was a future I could not envisage. Putting down my pen, still feeling a lack of energy, I ordered a meal from the adjoining restaurant. It was evening; the sun had gone down. Lake Rotorua shimmered, a cold, steel blue.

After finishing my meal, I looked at my watch. It was nine o'clock. I still had no energy for Nannette. I forced myself to get in my car and drive away, but when I came to the turnoff to Nannette's, my hands would only turn the wheel in the direction of home. Sadly, I followed this.

All the way back to Tauranga, memories were passing through my mind like a movie. I knew this was Nannette's last lap toward letting go. As I collapsed into bed, I asked for strength to help Nannette through the final stage of giving over.

Chapter 7

Her Final Breath

I was determined to see the sunrise across the water. I dressed myself; in the process, breaking the lace of my comfortable old trainers I hadn't wanted to let go of. While hunting in the wardrobe for the new pair I had been saving for happier times, the phone rang. I ignored it, feeling the importance of this morning's walk. I put on my new deep-blue trainers; the colour reminded me of Lake Rotorua.

Walking briskly as the sun tried to peep through the clouds, instinctively I started taking deep breaths; each time I inhaled the cold air, it generated confidence. At the point of the peninsula, looking down on the channel, I noticed the incoming and outgoing tides were meeting, creating whirlpools of conflict. It truly was a grey winter's day. The walking had warmed my body, and I returned home ready to face the new day.

The phone was ringing as I walked up the steps; it was Mike, and his voice sounded weak.

"Nannette's asking for you, love. Could you please come over? She missed your visit last night."

After a quick shower, I was on the road. Panic authorised me to drive beyond the speed limit. Reflecting on my many visits, I realised my energy had been linked to Nannette's all the way along. When I followed my intuition to withdraw and not visit, Nannette had also withdrawn. No more answers were needed; she had completed reviewing her life. This was her time of departure.

I took another deep breath when I arrived. Family were gathered, and the home was bathed in emotion. My breaths were detaching me from the surrounding sadness. I entered Nannette's room; she was conscious, peaceful, and calm.

"Please, dear, I want the spirit guide to talk to me over what is happening," she said.

This was my most poignant moment with Nannette. I didn't want to channel; I just wanted to say, "Thank you for being my friend. I will miss you."

Putting aside my personal feelings, I knelt beside the bed. Holding her warm hand, I asked, "Are you in any pain?"

"No, dear. Please—is your spirit guide there?"

I reached up to connect; many spirit guides were present, and then the most uncomplicated words were passed onto Nannette.

"Can you feel the love in the room?" a spirit guide asked Nannette.

Nannette quietly responded, "Yes."

"Follow it, dear one. You are dying."

"Is that all?" Nannette was obviously expecting something more dramatic than a quiet feeling of love.

"This love is your transport," the spirit guide said. "Hold on tightly. Don't let go."

"Thank you dear," Nannette said. They were her last words to me. She lunged forward in a choking fit.

I yelled out to Mike to phone the doctor. I felt she needed a morphine injection so that her passing could be peaceful. He didn't want to let go, but another gurgling sound from the bedroom prompted him.

The doctor arrived and gave her the only morphine injection she'd had throughout her illness. It worked; she relaxed immediately.

As Nannette peacefully went into a semiconscious state, her family moved closer to her, and I left to stay the night at a friend's house. Her only daughter, Lana, took my place by the bedside, deciding to read to her.

"What is the name of the book, dear?" Nannette said.

"It's called *The Journey*," Lana replied.

As she started to read from the first page, Nannette travelled peacefully and willingly away from the physical world she had experienced for fifty-four years.

Chapter 8

Arrival of a Star

While Lana was reading to her mother, my friend and I reminisced about Nannette's journey. At the moment of Nannette's release, a liquid blue light resembling a star arrived between us; feeling its presence, we both turned to look. The phone rang; Nannette had just passed on. My friend and I got into the car and returned to Nannette's house.

Parking in the driveway, I looked up at the sky through the huge rimu and pine trees growing on the lawn. There was Nannette amongst the stars. I could see her form covered in a garment of scintillating blue light. A spirit guide stood on each side of her, another in front of her. They were shaking her hand; all were dressed in the same blue garments of light. Not only could I see clearly, I could also hear what was being said.

"I have no clothes on," said Nannette.

The spirit guides smiled and embraced her. "You have left your physical clothes behind," said one.

"You don't need them anymore," said another.

I gazed at this phenomenon until they merged with the night sky. Elated after this experience, I walked inside where

I was embraced by Mike and Lana. Exhausted, relieved, and in grief, they offered me a drink.

"She didn't get her wish," said Mike.

Not knowing why, yet with great conviction, I answered, "She still will."

The gap Nannette had left was huge. I still felt connected, yet with no sadness, for her passing had filled this space with love. All those connected were feeling the harmony and peace of her transition.

I finally understood that the inner connection Nannette and I shared had just shifted its position to another dimension I knew was real.

Chapter 9

Nannette Appears

Many years had elapsed since Nannette's departure; I was divorced for the second time, but I had met someone new. His name was Deane. It was an off-again-on-again relationship and I didn't quite know where I was, yet I continued to work with spirit guides and help others.

During my last walk with Nannette, she had said, "It's not right. You are doing such good work. More people need to know about it. I'm going to do something about it." But then she died.

One night as I was thinking about all of this, Nannette appeared in front of me. She held out both hands; one palm was facing the sky, and the other was facing the ground.

She said, "As is above, so is below."

I understood this to mean that whatever is above eventually manifests. Immediately I picked up pen and paper, and with Nannette's voice telepathically resounding loudly in my mind, I started writing.

This part of the book is her story. Nannette's flow of words started with my name.

* * *

Gina, I have waited for you to have a quiet time on your own so that I could communicate with you. Destiny is eternal, and writing this is part of your destiny and mine. My wish was to help others know about spirit, and now I can. The biggest block in my earth life was fear of the unknown; I don't have this block now, which is why I can help. I wish you to write down what I say and put it into a little book to help others know there is a greater world out there. A world that not only cares about people's happiness, but a world that is filled with guidance and understanding over how to live life. This world is called spirit guides, and this is my experience with them.

My passing over wasn't traumatic because after I was given the morphine injection, my body relaxed. And as it did, I just arrived on the Other Side. I knew I was still alive for I could see and hear everybody. I looked down on my body, and it looked like it was sleeping; family were crying, so I tried to move back into my body to tell them I was still alive, but I couldn't. I travelled beside you to let you know, but you only felt my presence as a star; you couldn't hear me. Intense love surrounded me; I heard my name being called. At the same time, the love around me became so powerful a wave of it lifted me up, and I glided into the sky where you saw me with one male spirit guide in front shaking my hand, and two female spirit guides, one on either side of me. That is when you heard me say I have no clothes on. The spirit guide in front of me laughed, explaining how my physical body had clothed my soul whilst I lived my earth life, and now that I no longer needed it, a garment in the form of pale blue light had taken its place. You'll laugh at this, Gina. Immediately I looked to see if it was see-through, as I always imagined light to be transparent—it wasn't. The guide laughed again, saying, "You'll get accustomed to your new body." We then started moving.

Travelling fast, high above earth's atmosphere, safely surrounded by pale blue light—resembling a cocoon—I remained inside, a little scared of what lay ahead. I could hear the spirit guides talking to each other.

"Keep moving on," said one.

"Yes, she is not ready yet," answered another.

It was a little like being in an aeroplane; if you move with the surges at take-off time, your feelings are heightened. If you resist the movement, you create friction—the ride then becomes bumpy. My body started to adjust, and then I felt like stretching my limbs, moving them. It felt safe to do this; then the energy around me started to slow down.

"All right," I heard a spirit guide say. "We will stop now."

I could hear one spirit guide conversing with another at the place of arrival. Landing was the same as an aeroplane descending onto a runway. The difference being the landing ground wasn't tarmac; it was a huge circle of blue light narrowing into a passageway filled with white light. Where was I? I knew my life as Nannette was over—and that I was still alive—but I didn't think I would feel quite the same as I did on earth. Yet here I was in spirit land with all the same thoughts and feelings as I'd had on earth; the only difference was that my body felt lighter. I looked around for a mirror to see if I still looked the same; there wasn't one, so I moved on. Blue light was all around me, and even though I was unsure of where to go, this all-encompassing light seemed to be moving me along the passageway that was lit up with white light. It resembled the exit from the plane to the terminal at an airport on earth. Then I saw two spirit guides dressed in silvery-blue robes; they guided me into a spacious room filled with people. Smiling faces greeted me.

I wondered where I was, and then I started to recognise my mother, father, aunts, uncles, and friends I had known in my earth life; they all looked so young—no wonder it took time to recognise them. All were dressed immaculately, hugging and chatting to each other like they hadn't seen one another for a long time; it sounded like they were catching up on gossip. This scene resembled a wedding; the conversations were all about their own individual experiences. I could hear my father saying, "That is very interesting. I haven't been there yet."

Then my mother moved forward. The dress she had on was beautiful; it was covered in thousands of pale pink, pearl sequins. Embracing me, she said, "We know you don't want to wait with us, and although you were my daughter on earth, we all understand you are eager to follow your own soul journey; therefore I am delighted to see you for only a short time."

She went on to say, "Most of our journeys are very different; this is the wonderful freedom we have here. We can be ourselves. I work with others creating clothes that are compatible with a person's evolvement, where their journey is at. I love it. There are two thousand people in this room; I have designed most of their clothes. Unlike the slow process of using your hands to work with patterns and fabrics on earth, here it is very fast. First, spirit guides give me energy, which is similar to when people on earth get inspiration, then this frequency is transferred to my eyes, and as soon as I feel enough energy, I use my eyes like a laser to create a garment. I keep going until all the energy runs out; sometimes the clothes are created in one session, but most times it takes three attempts. During this time, I get to know the person's journey. Your clothes won't change until you reach your next destination. I can see your journey, and this is why I can understand your eagerness to move on. Look—isn't that one of your spirit guides over there beckoning you?"

I looked across the room; a spirit guide in silvery-blue robes was waiting for me. I was pleasantly shocked and surprised at this whole scene. Anyone on earth who thinks the Other Side is peaceful with no action is in for a surprise.

My mother hugged me again, saying, "When you have reached your destination, you will come back and visit my home. It is much nicer than the one I had on earth, gracefully positioned by a luminous, turquoise-blue lake, but I understand you have no interest in homes at present; you are waiting to move on."

She released her embrace, and I went straight into the arms of a spirit guide who turned me in the direction of the exit. I made it through the crowd and out of the exit. I had to catch my breath. Yes, Gina, you still breathe on the Other Side, and all I can say about this experience is—it was amazing. I was left elated. I knew I had to calm down before I went anywhere else, but it only took me a few breaths, and I was ready to start moving again.

Where was I going now? The same white light that had formed a passageway was present, but now it was merging into a corridor containing many doors. Although I felt safe, I was unsure of where I was, so I turned to communicate with the spirit guide that had ushered me out of the room. She had departed; I truly was alone, and even though this part of my journey looked alarming, love started to circulate around me. Then I remembered the words your spirit guide said to me as I was dying: *This love is your transport; follow it.*

Using my will, which interestingly enough was becoming stronger, as were my senses, I followed this feeling of love, knowing it was my guidance. It carried me along the corridor, stopping at the First Door. I knew I had to assess what was behind these doors; it felt like a test toward finding myself. With this guiding love around me, I didn't feel frightened. I was also aware that another spirit guide wouldn't appear until I had made it through to the right door.

The First Door looked clean and strong. I tried to perceive what was behind this square-shaped door, and as I imagined myself going through it, I felt myself moving backwards. I quickly realised this door must contain my past, so I moved forward to the next door.

The shape of the Second Door was out of perspective, crooked, and partially open. I could see religious symbols and statues stacked inside; it didn't take long to realise this was the door of my past religious concepts. I didn't need them anymore; my concepts were being replaced by real experiences. Happy with finally being able to experience spirit, I moved on to the Third Door.

The shape of this Third Door resembled that of my home on earth. Loved ones I had left behind were mourning for me inside this door; I could hear them. Moving forward to enter, feeling responsible for their grief, a gust of wind coming from nowhere shut the door in my face. I moved back, realising their grief was out of my control. I could not interfere; sadly, I moved on.

The Fourth Door looked interesting; multi-coloured artistic designs made the door look like an entrance to a temple. I knew many good presences lay inside this door. I felt around for the presence of love; it was moving between the door and myself. It started to open. I stood still, wondering whether to go through, and then a hand reached out, handing me a red rose. Around the rose, a gold light was forming the words 'homeward bound'. Then I saw a female spirit guide smiling at me. I knew this door had the records of my friendship with spirit guides and knew I'd entered this door before. I thought of you, Gina, as loving memories of when you first channelled a spirit guide to me whilst I was in my earth life flooded through me. I wanted to go in, but the love propelled me forward to the next door.

The Fifth Door was hard to describe; it was full of spaces. A different type of love was present, and as I moved closer, the door dissolved, becoming a landscape. I could feel a weird kind of love from inside this door; I had experienced love like this before. And, being curious, I took a step toward the landscape that was stretching far into the distance. A feeling of moving away from the love that was guiding me made me stop. Pulled in two directions at the same time, I clutched at the red rose; love gently turned me toward the Sixth Door.

The light from this Sixth Door was all-encompassing; love was felt in my heart as well as my mind. Trusting this feeling of love, I entered. The room was filled with spirit guides dressed in creamy, golden-coloured robes; one beckoned me to sit down. Huge, brightly coloured cushions in every colour of the rainbow were positioned on a floor of misty blue-grey light, resembling smoke.

"Welcome back, dear one," said a male spirit guide. His voice was familiar. He handed me a drink in a golden goblet; the contents were bubbling like champagne. Speaking slowly, he said, "This is what people on earth would call the Cup of Youth. It will renew you for it feeds the finer body of light you now reside within. Drink and rest. You will be ready to move soon."

"Am I travelling somewhere else?" I asked.

"Yes, your mind is your compass. It will direct you, and you do still have a mind."

"I have an appetite too," I replied. "I am very thirsty." As I drank from the golden goblet, it automatically kept filling up. Suddenly I thought, maybe I could become drunk!

"And lose your mind," laughed the spirit guide. "Overindulgence with alcohol on earth separates the mind from the physical body; your thirst is monitored here. This drink is designed to bring the particles of your new body back together; you are a little fragmented after your journey. When you feel at home, you will no longer have a thirst and need to drink."

As I turned to look into the smiling eyes of this spirit guide, I remembered seeing him in a dream whilst living on earth. His turquoise-blue eyes were flowing with compassion. Feeling safe, I just stared; then pictures of my earth life started to form in his eyes—and experience after experience was shown to me like a movie. As I was observing myself through his greater mind, I noticed that the parts of my earth life where I did well were shown first; then as I viewed my mistakes, they were shown with so much understanding and love I didn't feel bad—no judgement was present. I did feel embarrassed watching myself judge others. This was an eye-opener, because with every judgement I made, I could see my love disappearing. What was interesting were the times I had tried to understand spirituality; these moments were shown as a longer time in contrast to the efforts I had put into acquiring material possessions. Those times moved very fast, as if they were irrelevant. I viewed my entire life, saw myself dying and returning to an embryo, safely carried by three spirit guides inside a huge blue light until we landed, going through a corridor of white light, then entering the Sixth Door and arriving here to this place, which felt like home.

The female spirit guide beside me smiled. "Yes, you are home. It is not always a pretty sight to view oneself in the jungle (referring to earth). It is only when one is willing to face the good and bad times in their lives, with courage, that one can then see clearly."

What took years to live through on earth was passing before my eyes as moments.

"What was the purpose of the doors?" I asked.

Another female spirit guide moved forward saying, "People that don't believe or have no awareness of the afterlife before they pass over go straight to places within the soul plane that contain healing, and when they are healed and adjusted to passing over, they start their journey along the white corridor. Those with a belief in the afterlife are required to use their will and sense the direction they are moving toward. You did very well, but you have been through this corridor of doors many times before when you passed over from previous lives you have lived. I will complete your understanding of what they mean, and then we will travel to another destination."

"The First Door contained memories of your life as Nannette, and because you were aware of your soul's eternal journey before you died, it was easy for you to move on. This is the door many are stuck behind. On earth you call them 'earthbound souls'. They are truly suffering, and they wish to be back on earth with their loved ones. Much help resides within this door; you didn't need it, so you could move on.

"The Second Door was old knowledge that is now dead—yet many still live within this confinement. A lot of stubborn souls reside here—even spirit guides that used to be teachers. Some of them won't move on because they want the power they once had. You could say they are dark, but there was a time when they were full of light. These beings do try to trap people into listening to them. This is why one must always question guidance—if it doesn't relate to your personal journey, throw it out. Another way to test a spirit guide is the love they have for all of humanity. Ambition and ego, without love, is a sure sign of darkness. Darkness is not eternal; that is why it is stuck here within the Second Door. It can't move on. Remember, darkness is nothing to be afraid of; it is only absence of light, and every now and then this place is refreshed with light. And when this happens, many wake up and move on. You happily moved passed this door.

"The Third Door was the grief you are no longer responsible for. When one is grieving, they are going through the process of letting go. A good thing to remember is that one can never own another person; you can share with another for a time, but you can never own another soul. When you can give another freedom, you free yourself. You have learned this; you are not possessive.

"The Fourth Door is where your spiritual friends back on earth travel at earth's night time to converse with us. You travelled through this door many times when you were spiritually developing in your life as Nannette; it is the place where information is passed on. This door will always be open to you; guidance from within it urged you to move on.

"The Fifth Door was your test. This is the door of imagination or desire. To enter would have absorbed you for many seasons, for that door contains altered expression. It is the plane many go to, we call it the ghost plane for it is where nothing is real and nothing is unreal; anything can be played out from the lowest to the highest. When one is unfulfilled, they go there to complete their desires. Your strength helped you to move on; this was because you desired true purpose.

"This desire has led you here to the Sixth Door; healing has been taking place. Soon you will enter the Seventh Door where you shall be prepared for your next adventure. Your moments here have spanned three days of earth time; your funeral as Nannette is taking place on earth. Come, I will show you another view."

As this female being of beauty and light moved, her hands generated the same misty, blue-grey light as the floor I was sitting on. Then another corridor appeared, and we started moving along it.

Chapter 10

Release

As I glided beside this female spirit guide, the freedom of movement was wonderful. I felt tall and slim; on earth, I was short and stocky. Moving in unison with this spirit guide gave me the courage to ask her if she had a name.

"My name is Ladina, dear one. I relayed many messages to you through your friend, Gina, on earth. We must now move faster; time is not standing still. We have work to do."

I knew it was the spirit guide that had spoken to me in my life on earth. She had the same vibration; a tear of relief started to fall down my face, and I stopped to collect myself.

"Don't stop," commanded Ladina. "Allow the tears to flow; this is your door of release."

We entered a crowded room created in the shape of a temple. It was filled with light, except for the black ceiling. Thousands of people filled this room—men, women, children, even babies. All had their heads down, as if in prayer. I noticed my body looked like Nannette again, and the body of light I was experiencing had formed itself into a circle of gold light around my head, like a halo; the others in the room were all the same. Then, as Ladina moved to a platform on a stage, all raised their heads to listen. She said, "Dear ones, all of you present here are aware your earthly life finished its cycle three earth days ago; this is your room of release. As many of your loved ones mourn in sadness over their loss, we will rejoice in your homecoming."

Ladina raised her hands toward the black ceiling, emanating the same misty, blue-grey light, resembling smoke. As it spiralled up, the black ceiling dissolved.

I turned to a man next to me and whispered, "What is that smoke?"

"It is what dissolves the veil," he answered. "I was a psychic in London and have seen it many times; it enables you to see into another dimension. Look up there; isn't that your family?"

Even though my eyes were raised toward the now-dissolved ceiling, I was looking down on my own funeral. Tears flowed like a river as I observed the suffering of my loved ones through our separation.

A girl of about ten years of age moved onto the stage. As she raised her hands, she started to sing. The most glorious sounds I had ever heard resounded throughout the temple; one by one, each of us joined in—even me. Unlimited sounds were creating streamers of coloured light in the atmosphere, and these colours were travelling down to the people at the funerals on earth. I watched as the sadness inside my loved ones was transmuted into joy through these healing rays of light. I also observed members of my family becoming embarrassed at their lack of tears, not knowing that the streams of colour and light were removing their grief.

As the process continued, Ladina walked amongst us, answering questions. I asked why a child had initiated this healing.

"This is a master soul," answered Ladina. "She died at the same moment as you, from cancer. Her earth parents cannot understand why. They are very angry; they blame others."

"Why did she die of cancer?" I asked.

"Part of the reason is she gave love and it wasn't reciprocated. Her emotions were starved; this threw her out of balance. There are many reasons for cancer; the most common comes from the environment you live in. Many people are aware of the damage done from toxins in their environment, so they choose to live an environmentally healthy lifestyle as you did—and they still end up getting cancer. With these cases, if you investigate their lives, you will find their emotions weren't freely flowing. Their hearts and minds were not in sync—causing imbalance—the perfect environment for cancer. Learning to treat imbalances as an indication that a lesson is present should be the first step toward healing. All people living a life on earth are learning something; if these lessons were found and worked on, a person's health would get better. This is why doctors need to be trained in a holistic fashion.

"Good health is very complex, and sometimes the reasons why a person suffers can appear so unfair, yet every experience contributes to expanding one's soul. This is why living a life on earth is welcomed by most souls; even a short life achieves a lot. This child didn't have any lessons left to learn; it was her soul's time to depart. She chose cancer because this is one of the illnesses humanity is on the brink of finding cures for, but another disease will appear until the soul is acknowledged or included in the evaluation of physical well-being. What needs to be remembered is that physical life is only a temporary existence; it is your soul that is eternal. If you are in tune with your soul, the death of the body is not that big a deal, especially when you consider most go through this process many times. This beautiful child's parents were obsessed with keeping her alive; they had pulled strings to adopt her, as many others wanted to because of her stunning good looks. They are very concerned with possessions, and she was seen as one of their possessions. After spending a lot of money to make her well, they didn't want to let go of their investment. When they knew they had to, they lost interest in her. Of course, her soul knew all this before she incarnated, for she is soul-linked to these parents. Their souls are behind schedule with their journey; she was trying to help them catch up by reminding them physical life isn't permanent.

"As the time of her death drew near, they took their minds off her by engrossing themselves in more material ventures; they were not present at her departure from her earth life. Another part of the purpose of her passing was to teach them unconditional love. Many cycles must now be lived through before they can learn this. This master soul cannot wait for that time; it would cause her undeserved pain, she is ready to live on higher dimensions and doesn't need to reincarnate again. However, when they do reach a higher level, she will travel to communicate with them—and all will be understood. This will be at a later date, when they have learned more about love.

"Spirit doesn't blame or judge; it waits for people to learn—and then they can be shown more clearly where they have gone wrong. Nobody can be told, and if you try to tell a person what they are learning before they are ready, you will harm them by making them angry, which then makes it harder for them to find out. Remember, you can't own another soul or fight the will of spirit; she knew this, and gracefully accepted her short journey with them. When the sounds in this room stop, I will introduce her to you, for you have been her mother in a past life."

My eyes were fixed on this child; her long, flowing hair looked angelic. I found this situation enlightening. A master soul dying of cancer made the word karma a sin to conceive of, yet many people on earth believed illness to be the result of karma. This concept I had taken on proved to be incorrect; and when you think about it, if you consider a person's suffering to be their karma, it does become a form of judgement.

Ladina didn't add to my thoughts. "Come," she said. "I will introduce you to this master soul."

Chapter 11

A New Friend

When Ladina introduced us, only moments were needed for us to connect. I smiled, and the child smiled; both of us communicated like old friends. Ladina explained the metaphysics of how, while our physical bodies were dying of cancer, we had communicated on another dimension. This was one of my greatest realisations since passing over: the fact that one does not have to wait until they die to travel to higher dimensions. It is all to do with higher bodies connected to the physical body; when one learns how, one can slip into a higher body and communicate with loved ones whilst the physical body is sleeping. I know you told me this, Gina, but now that I can see it, I can believe it. Before, I couldn't envisage travelling away from my physical body, but the messages you gave me did help me adapt more easily. Thank you.

We were ready to move out of the room of release. I was at peace with my transition, but the child looked a little sad. Once again, the misty, blue-grey smoke emanated from Ladina's hands; instantly we were back inside the Sixth Door. As we sat back down on the soft, luxurious cushions, the same spirit guide that had given me my first drink handed the child a golden goblet, calling her Destiny.

Ladina turned to me and said, "Her name is now Destiny. You will understand it when you enter the Seventh Door. Look! Observe what is happening to her."

As Destiny drank from the golden goblet, her form was growing and expanding rapidly. What I observed was no longer a child—but a beautiful female presence with robes identical to the other spirit guides in the room.

Ladina said, "You have just witnessed what takes place when a master soul returns home complete. Destiny lived twelve lifetimes on earth, helping others to learn the eternal lessons of love. This last lifetime only lasted ten earth years, and because her parents could not overcome their obsession with materiality, she couldn't teach them. All is not lost; her withdrawal will make them think. Once her absence is felt, they will search for answers and find them. You were her mother in a previous lifetime where love was honoured. You gave every step of the way; no disagreements were experienced. You both have clean slates. Because of this, you are eternally in harmony with each other. This master soul will now become your teacher as you enter the Seventh Door. I will now depart to help others. Freedom awaits you both."

All the spirit guides then linked hands, forming a circle of light. Music was seen and heard as colourful, dancing light; when it reached a sound like a hum, we started moving. Ladina waved good-bye as Destiny and I entered the Seventh Door together.

Chapter 12

Freedom

The feeling of expansion within the Seventh Door is almost impossible to impart to you, Gina. The closest I can get is remembering the first time you channelled to me in my earth life as Nannette. As my mind expanded with the spirit guide's words, I felt the presence of my ongoing journey, which gave me an incredible sense of freedom.

Destiny immediately explained that any awareness of the journey frees the consciousness and allows one to experience freedom. She was now my teacher and every time I thought, she would answer my thinking. Going on to say that once freedom is attained it remains inside the consciousness forever, only denial of love can prevent it from expressing; and freedom resided here within this room because blocks on love had been removed. I remembered working on my blocks whilst I was dying. Wondering if I had cleared them all, I went to ask. Once again, Destiny answered my thoughts:

"If you hadn't cleared your blocks, you wouldn't be here; those with blocks on love can't enter the Seventh

Door. This dimension has many mansions; one room can be compared to a country on earth."

The magnificent beauty within this room expanded into a never-ending space where night and day were present simultaneously. Many stars surrounded us, many moons and many suns. I could experience the warmth of the sun at the same time sharing the peace of a moonlit, starry night. Spirit guides were everywhere; some were in groups, and others were peacefully communicating. All were wearing creamy, gold robes. None were in conflict, and they were leaving us alone. As I moved, I was blending with all surroundings. Turning to face Destiny, she handed me a huge ball of blue light to sit on.

"You are sitting on your soul," she said.

My concepts about soul made this 'sitting on it' most uncomfortable.

"Am I not my soul?"

"Not at the moment," she answered. "You are back in your spirit body, your eternal flame of consciousness; this is your true frequency. Your soul is between your spirit and your physical body; it clothes your spirit whilst you live a life on earth. It also activates when you travel into other dimensions. Your soul will now rest as you learn to blend with other frequencies. When you have learned to harmonise, without losing your own oscillation, you will be assigned as a helper for humanity, then your soul will become active again. People on earth who search for their destiny, travel to the outskirts of this dimension in their night-time excursions. Here they are met with the spirit guides that overlook them, and they take them into a healing room where they are dosed with the energy from their eternal flame. This aligns them with their destiny, and it is why, occasionally, a person on earth will go into a very deep, refreshing sleep and wake up happy. There may not be anything around them to be happy about—this is because they have absorbed a highlight from their future.

"When a person dies, it is not leaving their earth life that is sad—it is the unfulfilment that goes with them. If a person doesn't fulfil his or her destiny in a lifetime, it has to be restructured in this healing room, and then the lifetime has to be repeated. This grief is greater than being separated from loved ones. People struggle without a connection with their soul or their spirit. Your soul can be referred or looked upon as similar to your spirit—just a weaker version.

"Spirit is adventurous; it doesn't remain in a state of bliss. It travels, and its descent into physical matter is a journey it wants to experience. During this process, your soul forms the first clothes you put on. You are learning to help people align themselves with their spirit and soul, and once you learn, you will be able to cope with any plea for help. Your soul will be bathed in compassion before you leave this place. This compassion will form a garment for you to wear; you will then travel out as a spirit guide. This is the testing ground."

As I sat listening to my new teacher, I remembered the yearnings I experienced in my life as Nannette. My inner desires were coming to pass.

"How did I make it here?" I asked.

"Through your love for others," said Destiny. "Now I wish you to experience your own individual portion of love."

"Am I not feeling it now?"

"No," answered Destiny. "You are surrounded by a similar love; this is making you in love with love."

I laughed; all the spiritual concepts I had entertained about the afterlife meant nothing. This spirit guide was about to teach me to love myself—here, on this high plane. No wonder I had found it difficult on earth. I wish I could tell Mike . . .

Bang! I landed back on earth beside him, experiencing the coldness of his loneliness. I panicked, feeling like I couldn't breathe.

My new teacher surrounded me. "Back we go," she said. "You are not ready to give yet."

Chapter 13

Learning to Harmonise

Uncomfortably sitting back on this ball of blue light, my teacher advised me to relax. "It will expand as you learn," she explained.

I looked down at this fluid-like blue light; it was already expanding. "Where was my soul when I lived life in the body of Nannette?" I asked.

"It resided within a spectrum of blue light surrounding the earth's atmosphere, and this was connected to your earth body by a long streamer resembling a lighted taper, which monitored your physical heartbeat. This spectrum of blue light is called the soul plane, and this was the first place you entered at your departure time. Once you were in your soul body, you were able to move to the Sixth Door where your mind became purified in the room of release, and then you entered this Seventh Door. During this process, you connected with your spirit body; your soul will now reshape itself as you learn to harmonise.

"First we will show you how to blend with your own love, and then you will know your own individual frequency.

Contemplate the times in your life when you were truly happy, and as you do, exercise the feeling these thoughts will create—move with them."

As I did, love coursed through my mind, and I connected with a creamy gold cloth continually manifesting from a huge spiral into infinity. As this almighty movement slowed itself down, a portion of this cloth caressed me, forming the cream garment I was now wearing; it was the same as Destiny's. As this occurred, love transcended feelings. I was absolute within the Supreme Hand of Creation.

My teacher explained this experience: "It is necessary to be reborn when you reach this stage of the journey. Your soul is now purified or cleansed from all your past lives, including the life you lived as Nannette. Your past lives will now remain in the Hall of Records so that you are able to view them at any time. Would you like to go there now and view the many different masks you have worn?"

I chose not to because I was eager to move on with helping others I had known.

Destiny smiled, "Yes, what's in a face, always something you don't like; the face is a mask, very rarely is it a true representation of what's underneath. Perfection doesn't belong on earth, it does belong here. Take a look at your face now."

A mirror materialised in front of me. I could not believe how beautiful I looked. Although I did look different, I could see a hint of Nannette in my eyes and around my face. Destiny explained how individuality existed even on the highest levels, and the reason I resembled Nannette was that this was the life I had made the most progress; therefore, a hint of it had remained.

I asked her if some of the souls I had loved would recognise me.

"I am about to explain this to you," she said. "However, you need to understand that all your attachments with others have been transmuted into special tasks to complete. You won't feel like a wife, a mother, or a close friend to those you knew, but you will feel overwhelming compassion, yet without any attachment to them, this is why we have the Hall of Records where you can refresh your memory over whom a person was to you. You will appear as Nannette to those who knew you. We will now move back to the soul plane, which is closer to the earth. This is where spirit guides congregate to discuss how we can help a person's earth life. Come with me, your mission as a helper has almost begun."

Chapter 14

Nannette's New Clothes

We entered a spectrum of blue light in the shape of a spaceship filled with millions of spirit guides. Destiny and I went into a room on our own; it had a silver device like a telescope, and I eagerly looked through it. This is when I saw you, Gina.

"What is the picture you are looking at?" Destiny asked.

"My friend on earth; she is about to make a wrong decision. It will cause her pain."

"What do you feel?"

"An urge to stop her."

"Look over here. This is the map of your friend's life. Observe the destination. Now look at where she is."

"A long way from it," I replied.

"Yes, so what we are going to do is travel to her. When we arrive, I will teach you how to harmonise with her vibration."

As Destiny held my hand in a familiar way a mother does a child, she talked about destiny being an energy that all people are born with. And that every time a person made a decision that was in tune with their true destiny, this energy was released into the aura before it manifested as events in the physical life. She furthered my understanding by saying:

"Not many people fulfil their true destiny; this is why they reincarnate. It is mainly to fulfil the original destiny from their soul, and because soul isn't recognised as the life force behind physical life, most people get caught up in what they think they want, so they create a pathway different from what they have been born with. They oppose their soul's desires by not listening to their intuition. This creates unfulfilment, and karma is the result of this.

"Karma started off as a balancing lever inside the wheel of rebirth. When a person went off their pathway, it would swing in the opposite direction to bring them back into balance. It was never meant to punish; that suffering is created from ignorance of soul. Those who harm others are not linked to their soul, and when they pass over, they go to special dimensions that help to correct them. Yes, they do suffer, but most people don't commit horrendous crimes. Only a few fall low enough to entirely disconnect from their soul.

"Humanity's main suffering is coming to terms with the truth that their physical life is transient; without understanding the journey of soul, this can create a very negative attitude. Not growing old gracefully is part of this. Earth is lacking understanding of soul, which is why we are trying to reach people. Enlightening people's minds toward awareness of soul will raise earth's level; once this happens, people won't suffer so much. Your friend wasn't born with karma; she has created some through losing confidence in her own guidance. Let's get moving; she needs us."

After listening to Destiny's explanation, I finally understood the word karma; it was to help people balance their destiny.Arriving at a place that looked like a shopping mall, I noticed every shop was full of clothes. I thought of you, Gina. You always loved clothes, especially those with a French influence. I stopped at a shop where the clothes looked very French. I wanted to go in, but Destiny pulled at my hand. We travelled to the last shop at the end of the mall. The shop had a bigger door than the others; as soon as we entered, a spirit guide took us into a dressing room. Another spirit guide appeared as a wardrobe mistress and dressed us in our new clothes. Destiny's garment changed into a living gold robe, like a Greek goddess, whilst mine changed into a smart, glowing, light green skirt and jumper. I looked in the mirror and realised I resembled my physical form as Nannette. Gold light surrounded my green clothes.

"We are being dressed in fabric designed from spirit," Destiny said. "These clothes are our spirit's choice to appear within. It is better for you to remain as Nannette when you travel to those who know you. Recognition does wonders when fear surrounds a spiritual experience. You are adjusting well; now we can enter the slower vibration of the physical world, earth."

We arrived in your auric atmosphere to help you, Gina. Your head was in your hands, and you were crying. I wanted to console you so I moved forward.

"Wait!" said Destiny. "You must not give her love until she raises her energy to a higher frequency—or else you will blow the circuits in her auric field, making it impossible for us to help. Remember, you need to harmonise with her vibration, not overpower it. Wait until her mood lifts; it will, for she wants answers. Soon she will ask for guidance; when she does, her vibration will automatically raise itself. If you stand back, she will still feel your presence. Once she accepts your vibration, you can blend with her. As you harmonise, her own will to make the right decision is intensified through light. Because your friend is psychic, she will sense our presence more quickly."

It was so unusual for me to see you in this state; in my earth life, I was used to taking people to you for help. My perspective on you at that time was an evolved soul that had incarnated to help others; it was hard for me to accept you had your own personal lessons because the guidance you brought through was all-encompassing. This energy blurred my vision, and I did get you mixed up with the guide. Now I can help you. After about fifteen minutes of earth time, you started to raise yourself into a receptive state—and then you asked for help.

"What do I do now?" I asked Destiny.

Passing me a parcel containing pictures made of light, similar to photographs, she replied. "Give her these one by one. Feed them into her aura and wait for her auric field to absorb them. This may take time because if she doesn't like the feeling of her future, she will reject them—and we will have to wait for her to come round to accepting her true destiny. Feelings rule the aura; it expands and contracts with every thought and feeling. When each picture is accepted, she will settle into a peaceful harmony."

I noticed Destiny held one picture back. As I placed these pictures of light correctly, Destiny stood metres back from you. When I had finished, I asked her to explain why she was standing back so far.

"My garment is woven with threads of destiny," she said. "These threads contain past and future lives. If I move too close to your friend, she would feel a particular past life, and her heart would break."

"Why would it not enlarge her love of the future?" I asked.

"At this particular time, she is in love with the wrong man. Her mind is set on being with him; her tears are from his withdrawal. If I had moved closer to her, I would have activated a previous lifetime they shared love, and this would have made her have stronger feelings for him. It would confuse the guidance we are trying to give her. This life is different, yet her focus is so determined toward being with him that she is already tuning in to the love she shared in a past life with him. This is bringing it back to life and throwing her out of time. As she unconsciously draws on this past love, by thinking of him, she creates another cycle of disappointment to live through. Her destination lies in another direction—and so does his."

"Does this happen often?" I asked.

"Yes, many do this when they want a relationship with a soul mate that is not meant to be this time round. Personal love can be felt out of time. There are many soul mates; the right one enhances a person's purpose in this life. They help each other with whatever difficulties they are going through. This man has led her up the garden path; he doesn't care about her problems and doesn't want to know."

"But he seems to love her."

"He does—from a past time. It has no future in this life; this is her suffering. Real love does not give pain. The pictures she's now absorbed are steps toward becoming free of him; these will guide her. When she has completed each situation and is ready, we will return with the last picture. It contains the plan for her future. She will then have the opportunity to reach her true destination."

"Can I look at the photo?" I asked.

Destiny laughed, saying, "You already have. Come. We will return to the place where you viewed her true destiny; earth's atmosphere is beginning to dim your awareness.

Your friend is asleep now and has already left her suffering behind."

I know you are thinking about this, Gina, and wondering who the man is. It was Deane, and the guide explains your relationship in depth further on in the book. Keep writing, and you will get to that place.

Chapter 15

A Helper at Last

As we travelled back through the dimensions, we stopped at the shopping mall. Inside the shop, Destiny removed her garment. I followed, placing my clothes of spirit fabric into the same arms of the spirit guide who had dressed us. I had enjoyed wearing my green skirt and jumper and didn't really feel like taking them off. It's interesting how attachment spans higher dimensions as well!

"Don't worry," said Destiny. "You will be wearing them again. They are our work clothes. They will remain here as clothes for us to travel to earth in."

We left; this time Destiny was not holding my hand. I could manage the journey myself. Entering the Sixth Door, smiling faces greeted us. We drank from the golden goblets and then departed into an outstandingly beautiful scene within the Seventh Door. A never-ending landscape of rolling hills, adorned with gracefully positioned trees stretched out into the distance and blended with a scintillating, silvery-blue sky. Valleys with streams separated the perfectly placed trees; in the distance, snowy mountains stood tall as if they were overlooking the scene. Together they echoed a symphony of sound, and although quiet, when I liked what I was hearing, it became louder, rising and falling with my love of its harmonious splendour. Gardens of perfumed flowers were everywhere.

"Familiarise yourself with the surroundings," said Destiny. "This is where God talks to God."

I sat by a stream and ran my hand through the water. It felt like silk caressing me. I floated to the top of one of the snowy mountains, and I experienced utter ascendancy as I looked down over the scene.

Destiny arrived beside me, "This is the true meaning of being unlimited. Spend some time enjoying your attainment, bathe in a stream, and walk in the valleys. I will leave you to acquaint yourself with your new surroundings."

The stream sang to me. I walked in a valley; the silence was all-knowing. As I walked within this landscape of breath-taking beauty, love, and light, I reflected on how some of the surroundings resembled the scenery of New Zealand I had loved. Knowing this was now my home, I asked Destiny what my next journey would be.

"Your learning to be a helper is now complete. You will rest here and restore yourself. Then you will travel out to help those that suffer; their need will create your pathway. You are now a guide, like me. I will continue teaching on earth through your friend, Gina, with another name that belongs to my soul. Your name shall remain Nannette; we shall meet often in this garden of light with many other souls from all walks of life and countries on earth.

"This garden is a destination for all souls that have completed their cycles of earth lives. There are many other dimensions beyond this, but because these other dimensions don't relate to having an earth life, no one can enter them until they have completed the cycle of reincarnation on earth and arrived here. You have earned the freedom to travel to other dimensions beyond this, but you have chosen to remain here and help others complete their cycles of reincarnation. This garden is a timeless dimension; on earth, your loved ones are preparing for the time of Christmas. Gina's mother is preparing to pass over and join us; your first assignment is to help her transition. You have a lot of work to do; you are now free to be a spirit guide for humanity. Be happy; your wish has come true. It was your destiny."

Chapter 16

Farewell to My Mother

Wow! I stopped writing and put down my pen. Even though Nannette's life on earth had ended, her new journey as a guide had just begun. She was doing what she always wanted; the only difference was that it was all taking place on another dimension. My talks with her had just shifted from verbal conversation to telepathically communicating; although I had only seen her materialise in front of me a few times, her energy had lived with me throughout the months of writing down her experiences.

Now it was back to my own life. I expected to drop down without having Nannette's inspirational flows with me, but I didn't. Instead, life took on extra meaning as I studied my world within. What the spirit guide had said to me when I was sitting in the cafe by Lake Rotorua, the night before Nannette died, remained in my mind, especially the words: *Love is a multitude of fragmented thoughts and feelings, and analysing never gives you a true understanding of your life—your love does.* This new awareness made me study love, which entailed making time at the end of every day to reflect, not only on what I had done during the day, but more importantly if any love had been present. Interestingly, the days I did feel love, would give me a good night's sleep and I would wake up energised, excited to live through another day. Changing analysing my life to investigating if any love was present, gave me more energy.

My journey at this time was quite stable. The year 1999 ended and I had a lovely last Christmas with my mother. The following May she started remaining in bed during the day. My sister Wendy was looking after her, and she kept asking me to visit more frequently, convinced that our mother was dying. I didn't believe Wendy since Mum didn't have any particular illness and her mind was exceptionally clear. Most of all, I didn't get any feelings or premonitions about her. Then in the early hours of the morning, Nannette materialised in my bedroom—she even sat on my bed—so I raised my energy to tune in and listen.

"It is your mother's time to depart," she said. "And she stubbornly refuses to go. Her family here on the Other Side are all ready and waiting to transport her home. You must go to her and explain that her time here is up, and she is dying. Don't be emotional; just explain a little about the afterlife to her. Let her know she is ready for her next destination; I will stand by whilst you do this. Do it as soon as possible." Nannette gracefully moved away, leaving my bedroom filled with a very calm energy.

The next morning, I decided to stick with my own plans of visiting a friend—not because I didn't believe what Nannette had said, but I had found timing extremely difficult to pinpoint in my experience as a medium. Since my mother was so alive, I believed the timing was off. Yet when I arrived at my friend's, Nannette also arrived in my auric space with the words: *Go now. Go now*. She must have said it about six times. I didn't want to go so I ignored her presence, until, while having lunch under an almost bare apricot tree, an apricot came out of nowhere and landed in my coffee, spilling it all over my lunch.

"Where did that come from?" said my friend. "The last fruit was picked in February."

Fresh apricots were my mother's favourite fruit—this was the ultimate sign. "I have to leave," I said. "I think it is my mother's time to pass over."

I got into my car and drove off. When I arrived at Wendy's, Nannette was still with me; her presence calmed any hesitation I had. I sat beside my lovely mother whom I had never ever had a conflict with. "Mum," I said. "I think you are dying."

"No, I am not," she replied.

"Yes, you are; it's your time."

She lifted her head up, "Well, I didn't count on it."

This was difficult, so I thought I would try another angle. "Mum, Dad is there waiting for you."

"Well, I can't see him. I can see some of the others but not him. I am not going."

"Mum, it's lovely on the Other Side. It's a beautiful place. My friend Nannette is there. She's told me lots about it. It's better than living here."

She shot up in bed and said, "You're not thinking of going—are you?"

This was useless; I couldn't get through. I spent the rest of the visit telling her how much I had loved having her as a mother. She started looking very dreamy and, as I left, I realised the loving words had created the shift. I cried myself to sleep that night. In the morning, Wendy rang to tell me Mum was going into a coma. Her passing was peaceful; her four children and her favourite grandson, my eldest, were present. He even witnessed the blue-grey light, like smoke, come out of her mouth moments before she departed. Nannette's experiences had taught me this smoke was the power that dissolved the veil between earth and the Other Side. I explained this to him. It reassured him. It does help when you see something and you know what it means. When they carried her rather large body—from Irish and French parentage—out on a stretcher, it looked so small; her soul had truly departed.

Her funeral was amazing; rays of light were pouring into the small church while the minister was speaking. I remembered what the spirit guide had said about funerals and how these rays of light were filled with healing for loved ones left behind, so I opened up and absorbed them. I saw my mother dancing round the room with my father chasing her. I telepathically connected with him.

"Your mother won't stop dancing," he said. "She thinks she is still alive on earth, and I can't explain it all to her until she stops."

This was my English father, always trying to discipline her and us. Well, he didn't stand a chance. *Dance with her,* I mentally called out; knowing the only disappointment my mother had in her marriage was that he had never learned to dance. I took the chance that he had prepared himself for their reunion by practising. I was right; the last picture I saw that day was of them embraced in each other's arms, waltzing.

Nannette had helped me see this higher view of my mother's passing. It is so much easier to let go when you have some awareness; even just imagining what the afterlife is like helps awaken belief. The tears from others present at the reception reminded me of the unnecessary suffering we go through when we can't see beyond our earth life. To most, she was dead; to me, she was more alive than ever. It's true I couldn't cuddle her again or have a human conversation.

Just a minute! Attracted by my thoughts, she entered my space. I could feel her cuddling my aura. She could telepathically talk to me. I heard her say, "I am proud of you."

That night in bed, I thought that the harmony I shared with my mother was because we understood each other. Wouldn't this world be a different place if everyone tried to do this? Maybe one day, when we learn our lessons and stop blaming, this will happen. I started drifting into a well-earned sleep.

Chapter 17

Facing Myself

Fifteen months had passed since I had communicated with Nannette. Despite the first day of spring rendering its warm sunshine—nature's way of melting the cold effects of winter—it truly didn't matter. I was having a bad day.

For all the insights and understanding I had experienced from communications with spirit, my human life was at a low ebb—emotionally and financially. My relationship with Deane was over. I had met a new man who lived in a different city. We had started seeing each other, but I hadn't heard from him for weeks. Nothing in my life was moving. Where was I going wrong? I questioned whether I should put my house on the market since I couldn't really cry poverty when I owned a house in an upmarket area by the sea, but I couldn't get any direction.

Spring was my favourite season, yet I could feel no joy. I had the flu, and my body ached. If I lay down, I would just keep worrying over my financial difficulties. Looking at my garden I had once so loved and cared for, observing how overgrown it had become, I attempted to weed it. Exhaustion overwhelmed me. I couldn't discern whether it was the flu or the memory of the many hours I had spent in this garden of twenty-eight years that was now such a mess.

I went inside and made a hot drink of fresh ginger, manuka honey, lemon, and garlic. Sipping it, I reflected on what I'd written from Nannette about the afterlife. I remembered the hours I had spent writing—sometimes until two in the morning—then getting up early to organise and drive my two youngest children to school. Sometimes words would keep coming into my head, and I would have to stop the car to write them down or ask my daughter to write them while I kept driving. I was addicted to pens and paper; they were my constant companions. Yet, I was never tired; now I was too tired to even weed my garden. I reflected on Nannette's garden of light. Her garden sounded heavenly in comparison to mine.

I looked out at the remaining flowers. My garden had once sparkled with masses of fragrant flowers in spring. Memories overwhelmed me, and tears started to fall. The more I cried, the closer I was moving, in my mind, to the garden Destiny had taken Nannette to. Then all of a sudden, I was *there* on a higher dimension. Nannette was looking at me, smiling.

My mind automatically went very calm and still from the change in energy. I was aware of her uplifting presence and the power from the spirit guide standing beside her. I picked up my pen. The spirit guide glowed in gold light; her emanation synchronised with my mind. For two hours, I was removed from my present problems.

She said, "My name is Lalesha; I was Destiny in chapter 11. You have reached another plateau in your mind, a state of higher altered consciousness whereby we can communicate. When people on this earth realise the potential in raising the mind to a higher frequency, the solving of life's difficulties will happen every day—then this world will change. To sell your home may seem a simple venture involving money, but it is not. You started a family in this home; your love and inspiration is woven into the structure of your older children's emotional makeup. They are attached—even though they do not wish to be. They want you to have happiness. Some attachments can be spiritually beneficial; others can hold you up.

"Selling your home here would solve your financial difficulties, but it would stall your soul's progress. More learning can be attained whilst you remain living here; also, you can't get rid of the past through moving away. It goes with you. You need to understand your life and unravel what was painful. Moving would make those experiences harder to access; you would be full of congestion from the past and unable to feel the genuine love flows that are underneath all your pain.

"Your children's love overlooks your human life—just as your love overlooks theirs. They are waiting to see if this new man you have met is sincere. Your disappointments with personal relationships are a worry to them; their faith in your love life is low."

"What can I do?" I asked.

"Know yourself," she replied. "Understand your different bodies, your flows and expressions. When you know and believe in yourself, you must go through a time of trust. Trust bridges the gap between an old cycle and a new one."

"Lalesha, is it not enough for you to just tell me my destiny? When I do a reading, other guides willingly tell my clients their destinies."

"No! Then you will just put it on a shelf and wait. Waiting delays destiny. Life is for living."

"But I have no money to live life!"

"You don't need money for what you are about to do. If you had money now, you would not do this writing, would you?"

"I guess not, Lalesha. But as a solo mother, some days I work 24/7. Don't you think I deserve a break?"

"A true rest is peace of mind—then one can relax. Your holiday awaits your completion of this cycle."

Starting to generate some faith in my future, I began to relax. I questioned this feeling. "Lalesha, whenever I contact spirit, I always feel warm and fulfilled—and any worry over my financial pressure goes. I don't even feel the need for a man in my life at these times. When I feel like this, am I in a state of fantasy?"

She immediately said, "When you tune into spirit, you start feeling the energy of your future, because the past and the future are known by spirit. The plan of your new cycle resides here in this garden with me. This energy is called your destiny, and it is connected to you by a thread. This thread is there to guide you. If you do not fulfil the steps left over from your old cycle, you will block your new cycle from coming in, and this warm feeling will depart until another incarnation. This is when you can call it a fantasy, but if you work hard to clean up your past, you will make room for the new—and then it will become a reality. Much work must be done for you to achieve your new cycle. Writing is part of it."

These words rang true. Contemplating the effort I would have to put into more writing, I started moving back into my human self. Before separating from the spirit guide, I called out, "Lalesha, where do I start?"

"Take my hand, and I will change your life. Consider me your teacher and for a short time, write it all down—then live it. Be honest to yourself, and you will be set free."

“Free for what?”

“To love again. Love is all that ever remains.”

Dropping back into my human self, I realised, if I was honest, I was too tired for love. I couldn’t feel any personal love in my heart, mind, or body. The memory of love enabled me to imagine and believe in it, yet I couldn’t feel it; therefore, how would I know if it existed with this new man I had just met? His name was Cliff; not only did we have an intense attraction toward each other, but an enormous peace surrounded us when we met. It made me feel at home with him—something I had never felt with any other man. *Well, I can’t meet up with him feeling like this, with no love in my heart. My human need for love might deceive me once again. This spirit guide has left me with a strong desire to be free of my past. Who knows—he could now be my past!* I mustered up the energy and made the decision to once again expose myself to a higher viewpoint.

“We start tomorrow,” echoed the guide.

“That quick?”

“The sooner, the better, for if you are not clear when destiny calls, then your old cycle becomes part of your new cycle—and you are never there.”

“That’s exactly how I feel, Lalesha. In fact, I have felt like this for a long time.”

“That’s because you haven’t had the time to face your own life. You have been too busy helping others. Don’t worry. This time you will get there—we are making sure of it. As you clean up your past, you will make way for your future. Freely become a child again and allow me to be your teacher. We can disagree, but understand that arguments belong to the earth’s consciousness. I will withdraw if the going gets tough, for you can’t coerce me into giving you what you think you need. I don’t want you to use your own wisdom. I need you to relate to me from the human you because not only is this the part that is receptive to my help, it is also the part of you that is learning. Become a child again, it will prevent you from getting carried away and overlooking some of the lessons I will take you through. I'm going to take you through a series of understandings to help bring your inner and outer life closer together. When your sleep state shares your living days, you become a living soul. This means your sleep state will be just as important as your physical day. Feel the love we have for you—and do your best to honour it. Freedom awaits you. I now depart."

Adjusting my schedule, I determinedly made a time for this most interesting spirit guide to speak with me each day. I had spent years as a medium, helping others. This spirit guide was concerned with my life—whereas the other spirit guides I had worked with were concerned with other people's lives. I knew it would be difficult to become a child again and ignore the wisdom I had absorbed from spirit guides over the years. The reality was that 2000 had come and gone, but my personal life was not moving. Whatever the reason, the clarity around this spirit guide felt like a new energy for the twenty-first century; therefore I was willing to let go of any knowledge I had gained and become her pupil for the sake of achieving my new destiny cycle.

Most spirit guides have experienced life in a physical body. This is why they have so much empathy for us. I could feel her compassion for my life; and as she withdrew, I didn't feel disconnected since another door in my mind had opened. To remove the past and only be left with the benefits appealed to my love of inner growth. The stage was set for me to achieve freedom from my old cycle.

Chapter 18

My Emotional Body

After a restless night of continuous waking, I woke up exhausted. It was as though layers of me had been exposed during the night. I felt vulnerable, even fragile. During breakfast, I contemplated yesterday's visitation from the spirit guide. My interest in what she had said gave me enough enthusiasm to try to contact her. I quickly organised the kids, drove them to school, and rushed home to start communicating.

Putting all wisdom I had learned to one side, feeling the child within—as my human sensitivity and frailties—I asked Lalesha for the first step on the road to freedom. Tears welled up in my eyes from her compassionate presence. I tried to ignore them, yet this emotional reaction continued pulling me into a depression that I didn't want. The moment I thought of the word *depression*, Lalesha overlapped my thinking.

"Depression is a result of not flowing with your destiny. When you ignore suffering and just keep going, depression begins. It is a normal function that kicks in when one needs to face life. Depression also happens when the soul has no expression. Your soul cannot breathe because your emotions are packed with pain and suffering created by disappointments and knockbacks on your road of life. The first thing we need to do is clean up your love life."

"I haven't got one, Lalesha. I am emotionally dead!"

"You say this, but when your emotions are healed, your soul case will open and love will start flowing again. You need to understand your different bodies and their flows."

"But it's hard enough to care for my physical body. It's always getting sick."

"It wouldn't if your other bodies were integrated and flowing. They would nourish your physical body. When one is cut off from these flows, the physical body takes the full load—and this pressure is too much for the poor old physical body. It was only meant to serve as a vehicle for your soul for a short time. It can't handle your eternal journey and your blocks. You must take responsibility and understand your knockbacks—and then it will function better."

As Lalesha relayed these words, my heart started to ache. I rubbed it for relief.

"You are feeling the tender loving centre of yourself," she said. "This is the doorway to your soul. Every painful experience you have been through has affected this tender, sensitive you. You would think your soul would be destroyed by now with all this harmful energy. However, it is not, for covering your soul is a casing called the emotional body; this protects your soul from being harmed. The layers that surfaced during the night were from your emotional body. They are now exposed and ready for you to investigate. Your emotional body is so packed with pain it must be cleansed and cleared before you begin a new cycle. This body of emotion can be looked upon as a vehicle that absorbs the impact of life's pains, shocks, and disappointments. You can compare it to a shock absorber; it takes the impact and can become worn out. When this happens, your physical body suffers. Your soul resides behind this body of emotion that needs to be cleansed and cleared so your soul can breathe. When your soul breathes, you are released from the past."

I breathed in this information; I knew it was true. My emotional body did feel heavy in contrast to my light physical frame.

"Where do I begin?"

"Start looking at your life without blaming others; confront your feelings, your past."

"I thought I'd looked at my life. I knew it was wrong to blame, and I didn't think I did."

Lalesha continued, "You don't outwardly blame, but when you include what has gone wrong in your own life to another person's actions or lack of action, you are blaming in a way. Sometimes too much insight when one is young can be a handicap. For example, as a young child, you could see the inner and outer personalities of people. You would see one of them in darkness—and then another version of them glowing in light."

"That's right, Lalesha. I could see two of everyone—uncles, aunts, family, friends. I liked the lighter version better; as a child, the darker version frightened me."

"Yes, this is the insight I am talking about. It created a lack of trust in others because you didn't have the maturity to understand others' journeys. To overcome it, you learned to put yourself in their shoes. This wasn't bad; it gave you understanding over how or why friends would do certain things, but it would also expose their thoughts to your psychic mind. Sometimes they would feel guilty, embarrassed, or even angry at your ability to know what they were thinking. You didn't want them to suffer any embarrassment, and you didn't want their anger—especially if you loved them—so you would ignore their dark side and concentrate on their light. This made others feel good. You were actually giving them a healing. And even though your ability to see their light was a good thing, you started tolerating too much from people because you didn't acknowledge their dark sides. Then, when you'd had enough, you would stop loving their light and blame what went wrong on their darkness. Everyone has a dark side; it is where their lessons reside. It is difficult to trust others, especially when you never know when a person's karma is going to kick in. If you don't acknowledge the negative energy created when a person refuses to face their lessons, they can hurt you."

"Is this the heaviness in my emotional body?"

"It was the beginning of it. When you entered your first relationship, and the other person couldn't meet up to your expectations of them, you simply loved the light within them. This caused both of you pain."

"I thought I was helping others by seeing and loving their potential, their souls. How could this cause them pain?"

"Yes, there are times when you can stimulate a person's connection with their soul by concentrating on the light in their eyes, but every human being on this earth has limitations to overcome. This is why they are here—the same as you are. If you had no lessons to learn, you would be blessing some other dimension. You have loved their light and ignored the reasons why they were living a life. It is wrong to ignore the negative parts of a person because this is what they are here on this earth to overcome. Most people are aware of their weaknesses; they hide them from others and secretly try to change. You caused them pain by ignoring what they individually had to go through. When you love a person, you must also acknowledge the level they are presently on—and treat their lessons as something sacred, not dark or evil.

"Most darkness is caused from suffering; it can become evil if it is left unattended. Many psychics have difficulty with this. A good psychic helps a person face what they are here to learn. They don't judge others' darkness; they help them remove it. You didn't judge, but as a child you were frightened of it—and you saw it as a threat to the light as an adult. It is not; light is eternal, darkness is temporary; there will come a time when it won't exist. Let other people deal with their own darkness. If they ask for your help, assist them; and if they don't, withdraw. All people struggle with what they are learning; it is part of living in a world that is evolutionary. Overcoming lessons helps the soul to grow.

"Relationships serve as one of the best ways to learn lessons. A good relationship happens when both partners can understand the other's problems. Also, the karma their partner is going through doesn't disturb their own emotions; they can handle their partner's down times with ease. Compatibility is imperative if a relationship is going to last; this happens if both partners are on a similar level. You have had partners that were going through lessons that were outrageous to you. You ignored their karma, hoping their personalities would change. It couldn't, because their dysfunction was a direct result of not facing themselves.

"There are many levels or types of love. Your difficulties have been enlarged because you have moved through your levels quickly. The men in your life have stayed on their own levels and been quite happy to simply just be themselves. You continued loving the higher aspects of them, and you felt rejected when they stubbornly remained on their level. You did not have the courage to say, 'My love has changed;

therefore I cannot share anymore'. Instead, you tried to change them. It is the same with friendships, when you outgrow them you must move on. You can still be nice, but don't relate to them on a heartfelt level. If you do, you will be constantly let down when they don't meet up to the level of friendship you're trying to share. With the men in your life, you continued loving the higher them; when this didn't work, you would obtain the courage to leave and let it fall away for the sake of love—even though it was unequalled. This has been your pattern for a long time. When you eventually did leave, you felt guilty. Guilt poisons the emotional body."

"But, Lalesha, I had children!"

"If children grow up with parents that do not love clearly, they will begin life unclear and hesitant over what they wish to do. Eventually their emotions will become congested. Parents need to be adults. An adult is one who strongly embraces change with responsibility. This comes back to accepting lessons as part of one's spiritual journey. If one partner doesn't acknowledge this journey, you have imbalance with the relationship. This is when separation is inevitable. Compromising one's beliefs doesn't work. You have suffered from imbalance; as you face your life, a new balance will occur. First you must use understanding and thoroughly dissolve the past structures you have created. Your emotional body will heal as you do this. Cast your mind back to the first man you loved. What do you remember?"

"Goodness. That's a long time ago. I was working three jobs to save toward travelling. One of these jobs was as an usherette at a theatre. One evening as I walked to work for the early session, I stopped at the corner dairy to buy a drink. Without thinking, I picked up a book and bought it. I was a few minutes late to the theatre and just managed to show the people waiting to their seats. *Doctor Zhivago* had been playing for weeks, and I was sick of seeing it. I sat down on the steps, and realised I had a book in my hands. The book was about understanding star signs, by Maurice Woodruff, an English clairvoyant and astrologer. Why on earth I had bought this, I did not know. Even though throughout my childhood I had experienced dreams that had come true, at that stage I didn't believe in a God, religion, or anything paranormal. I was into freedom of thought and equality for humanity. Yet, something made me read it. Turning to the chapter about my own birth sign, all my cynicism departed. It was so accurate. I couldn't put it down. The understanding put me on a high. I walked home that night too energised to catch the bus; I was not even frightened of the sometimes dangerous streets. I felt protected.

"The next morning, something inside of me had changed. I had connected with my psychic journey, and this small book had started me off. My day job was a beautician in a pharmacy; within two weeks, I had convinced the three chemists and the two sales assistants to believe in astrology. Friends started taking me to lunch so I could help them with their problems. Answers flowed through my mind easily. The little book had triggered my ability to see into people's lives. My life was going really well—and then I fell in love. He was the correct astrological sign that was compatible with mine. We were both very happy—until he dumped me all of a sudden. I was a sensitive Cancerian; it shattered me."

The spirit guide said, "I know, I have the records in my hands. What I want you to do is honestly look at how you constantly changed during those years. Would he have been right for you five years down the track? Take a look."

"No. He had a different dream than I did. When we met, he didn't want children—neither did I. Three years later, I did."

"Then how could he hurt you? He actually saved you from greater hurt."

"Yes, Lalesha, he did. But at the time I did not want a future without him. Something inside of me knew he was wrong, but I didn't want to let go. I was young . . . just a minute, Lalesha, I looked at this years ago, it can't be affecting me now!"

"Yes, you did let it go a long time ago, but what you didn't consider or understand at that time was the power of your mind. Thoughts create dreams that end up as mindsets of how the future is going to be. If these dreams don't manifest, not only does the emotional body suffer through being let down, your subconscious stores these unfulfilled desires and they become blocks that influence your future. Even though you moved on, you didn't dismantle the dreams you created. You just pushed them to one side, and this left you unfulfilled and sad. Even your first marriage didn't remove the emptiness; you did love him, but this feeling deeply centred in your emotional body led you to leaving him and marrying your last husband."

"What! I thought both marriages were guided. I had beautiful children."

"Not everything in life is destiny. Take a look back. Your second husband resembled the man you first loved: same colour eyes, same height, and same sense of humour. You simply replaced your past unfulfilment—or your emotions did. Many do this unconsciously; they attract the same type of person time and time again. If you are honest, you still like those looks. Don't you?"

"Lalesha, you are right. But it must be deeper than that; I can't believe I was just attracted by looks."

"Of course it goes deeper. You have been soul linked to every man you have loved, but it wasn't necessary to love them so deeply and want the relationship to last. What triggered the attraction with the first man you loved was a life in Italy where you were a nun and he was a wounded soldier. As you attended to his wounds, your eyes met each other and a spark ignited a desire for love. Both of you created a dream that couldn't be fulfilled at that time, so it transferred itself to this life.

"Energy can't be broken down; this energy of love only had enough power to last a short time. It wasn't meant to continue, but you created a mindset of it lasting. The love from that past life made him appear exceptionally good-looking when you met; most people shine when they are in love. You have held onto the memory of him shining. When you love another person, you must accept it has a time. This stops you from creating dreams that can't be fulfilled. In a way, it is practising unconditional love; however, you can make your mind think in an unconditional way, but not your emotional body, it needs more understanding. One can't make their emotions behave; they have to be unravelled gently.

"It is not always necessary to know what occurred in a past life before you can remove any pain from the emotional body. Whatever happened then usually has a corresponding lesson in this life. Your lesson with your first relationship was 'confidence'. You are still learning this; many people have this lesson to learn. If you would've had more confidence in your own ability to love, you would have stood back and observed how much love he was giving you. This would have shown you it wasn't enough to keep the relationship going.

"Of course he loved you, but he had used up his portion. You wanted it to last. I observe many people keep on loving when the flows aren't equal; relationships like this are needy and require constant feeding. When you think about it, loving another when they don't return the flow is stupid. It's wasting good energy; until this is realised, the emotions go through hell. When you are conscious of *why* you love a person, your emotions respond more clearly because this logic prevents you from wanting love at any cost. You don't get into difficult situations; this is the first step toward becoming confident. Being honest also helps this process.

"As you confront your past with honesty, the pain created from unfulfilled dreams will go. True love does not give pain. You released him from your subconscious in the night; this first layer has finally moved off. These layers remain in the emotional body until they are confronted. Every interaction you experience with another—involving love—goes into the emotional body. This is why all attachments must be seen clearly before they can be released. This freedom will increase as you view the men you have loved."

"Well, that should be easy, Lalesha. I haven't loved many compared to most people I know."

"You have loved enough to make your emotional body a huge throbbing sore. When you love deeply, greater energy is released from the soul. Other levels come into play, including past lives. Sex is a force that releases energy; however, sex should be the release of love—not the craving for it. A craving for love occurs when the emotional body isn't functioning correctly due to being too full or too empty. When the emotions are flowing and clear, sex goes to another level. It becomes the release of love—not the craving for it. Any craving for love indicates a block is present. As you look over your past relationships, see if you were craving love."

"I don't feel I was."

Be honest—yes, you were. It is the normal level or attitude on this planet—it is nothing to be embarrassed about. But now you want something better; you will achieve this if you keep moving forward. But first, you need to clear your emotional body, then your own love will return—and you will be free to love another. You will have confidence in your own ability to love. Tonight, before you go to bed, cast your mind back to all those you have loved. Compare the love you had for them with how your love is now—include what you love doing and where you want to be in the future. Honestly confront the compatibility of your past loves, and we will speak of attachments tomorrow. Don't become so focused on the lack of love in your life. Try to fly a little higher into the realms of love where dreams can be realised. As you go through this time, remember that your night-time excursions will be as important as your daytime living. They both will help you achieve freedom."

After this communication, I knew an unfulfilled dream was somewhere inside me. This spirit guide was going to help me remove the dreams that weren't right for my future. I couldn't lean on her. I had to cooperate and work with the information myself. Today she had raised me into feeling something lay ahead—and that something echoed freedom. What this spirit guide was saying was acceptable to my consciousness.

Before I went to bed, I did what she had asked. One by one, I cast my mind back to all the men I had loved. Using honesty and logic, I compared the level of love experienced then to how different I was now. It felt like popping balloons; the emotional memory was defusing in front of my eyes as I looked. Only the last two remained in my mind as I travelled off on another interesting night-time excursion.

Chapter 19

Viewing a Past Life

I awoke this day exhausted. Lalesha had called my emotional body a throbbing sore; well, that was exactly how I felt today. The flu was still present, so after dropping my children off at school, I decided to go to the gym; maybe then I would be able to tell the difference between the emotional pain Lalesha had talked about and flu pain by testing my body's physical strength with exercise.

While moving through the varied exercises, I dreamily started thinking of the last relationship I'd experienced before I met Cliff. It was Deane; I couldn't get him out of my mind. In fact, the memory started reaching such an intense feeling that the gym became a blur of machines and people. Removing myself from the rigorous activity of exercise I went into the sauna to meditate.

Lying down I started to relax, and stopped thinking of him as the dry heat of the sauna started to caress my aching body. Pictures flooded my mind. I imagined I was in the sun on a Caribbean beach. Oh no! Deane was there in my mind again, blurring any clarity I was trying to obtain. Intense pain started welling up in my heart, but I did what Lalesha had said. I tried to look at the level of love that had linked us together, by using logic. It was hard, as our relationship was a rollercoaster ride. He wasn't interested in my problems; every time a mere hint of responsibility entered the scene, he would disappear. I became used to his apologies; I would justify his behaviour by accepting that a solo mother with two children was a huge responsibility. I even pushed aside my own knowingness that children give more love than adults since they are freer—and it can be an honour to share with them.

Deane had never had children, and I was a mother of five; the three older ones had left home but periodically came to visit. He had loved the children, and they had loved him. What went wrong? I was going round in circles, feeling worse. *If only Lalesha was around now.* Immediately, she arrived.

"Telepathically talk to me," she said.

"Here in the sauna?"

"Yes."

Luckily, no one else was present. "Can't you read my mind?" I asked.

"Yes, but it is a blur. I want you to formulate the words clearly in your mind and then telepathically relay them to me."

"Lalesha, I cannot get Deane out of my mind. It's ridiculous—we broke up a year ago. These pictures are making me question if I've gone against my destiny. I finished with him because of his unstable way of living, but if I compare him to my life now—like you told me to do—many things I love, he loves: music, the sea, he is even writing a book. I don't want this pain I'm feeling; can you help me see him more clearly?"

"You are still attached by a small thread, and this blurs your vision."

"How can I clear this? And can you explain more about this thread?"

"All people are linked to a soul group. When you entered your first life on this planet, you came in with others of your soul group in a flow of threads that kept you connected. He belongs to your soul group, and your attachment with him in your past lives has mainly been as father and daughter—this was the pattern of most of your lives with him. However, one particular life connected your love on another level, and this is the attaching thread you have been dealing with in this incarnation."

"Tell me about that life please, Lalesha."

"He was a fisherman on the Caribbean coast. He was your stepfather; he loved telling stories, and you loved listening. You would remember these stories, write them down, and show him. The link was on a creative level and very intense. You kept a diary, changing the stories into romantic novels. Then one day when your mother was cleaning up, she found them. Your stepfather was a lot younger than your mother, and—in her insecure state—jealousy cast suspicion on a level of love that was pure. A fight began, ending in you leaving home. You went into the city where, destitute, you worked as a prostitute. Psychologically, the impact of your mother's thoughts degraded your level of love with your stepfather and damaged your perspective on love. You were an impressionable fourteen-year-old. You worked like this for four years, hating yourself and thinking of him often.

"Growing up without a father until the age of ten had made those four years where he was your stepfather the happiest years of your life. The stench of sweat from men, after sex, would remind you of the times at home when you would run down to the beach waiting for your stepfather to return after a fishing trip; as all the fishermen moved past you, the smell of stale sweat from days at sea emanated from them. This was once a happy memory. Much money was made by your profession as a prostitute. You lived in an elite apartment overlooking the water you loved. Your hair had changed colour and your body was fuller. Then one day as you were waiting for your next client, you looked in the mirror; your face was unrecognisable—you had changed. Regardless of what you were doing, you liked the look of yourself. You prepared the bed. Hand-embroidered covers of mauve, gold, and cream covered your wooden Spanish bed. Many paintings by artists who were your clients covered the walls. After bathing in perfumed oils, you sat waiting for your next client. He walked in. It was your stepfather. Now before I tell you anymore, you must go have a cold shower. This sauna is cooking you."

The shock of the cold shower was equal to the shock of these words. I was so caught up in this world of my past life that I didn't want to go home. It was lunchtime and the changing room was empty; I pulled out my pen and paper and started writing. As Lalesha spoke to me, I could see the events as pictures in my mind.

She continued, "You were so skilled at using seductive energy; not recognising you, this man fell at your feet. As he caressed you, a fire started to burn within you. Your desire for him was greater than his need for you. Passion exploded in relief and tears."

"Why are you crying?" he asked. "I am so sad myself."

"He went on to tell you he had been in the city for two years. His wife had died, and he was looking for his stepdaughter who had run away from home.

"I am a fisherman," he continued. "I only have enough money to last another month. If I go home without finding her, I will never forgive myself."

You immediately answered, "Stay here with me."

"You had saved enough money to live on for another two years. You stopped working and formed a romantic, sexual relationship with your stepfather. Then one day when you were cleaning out your wardrobe, a teddy bear dropped out. It was the one he had given you for your eleventh birthday. He rushed to the wardrobe, throwing clothes all over the room. Then he found the writings you had kept. Blazing with anger, he hit you until you bled—and then he left, spitting on your body as he slammed the door. You lay there for hours, bruised and in shock, then phoned a doctor who had been your first client four years previously. Do you want a break, dear one?"

I was certainly feeling the child within today; quietly I answered "Yes. If I go to a peaceful place, will you come with me and continue?"

"Yes. Go by the water; it is inspirational."

After dressing, I bought some lunch, found a quiet spot by a harbour close by and continued communicating with Lalesha.

"The doctor was your first husband in this lifetime. His interest in your creative ability, even after you both divorced, goes back to that past lifetime. After dressing your wounds, the doctor noticed your stories scattered on the floor. He started reading them whilst you slept. When you woke up, he was still there. He counselled you, convincing you to close the door on your four years as a prostitute."

"I have a friend in New York," he said. "He owns a paper; if you can write like this, then you could work for him. Nobody would know your past. I will lie; I will tell him your family have all been killed in a tragedy."

"The doctor made the way for a new life for you."

"Lalesha, my first husband is still my friend. It is interesting that in this lifetime he always encouraged me to write."

"There are parallels with every life," she replied. "He will always care about you because he is part of your soul group, but he is on a different journey to you at present."

"Have I met the one to journey with me?" I thought I would get this in quickly and trick the guide into telling me my future, but it didn't work—she just continued.

"On another level, yes, but you have more to go through yet before you can see clearly. Now, in that past lifetime, the owner of the paper and the doctor were close friends—and the owner of the paper became your husband in that lifetime."

"Lalesha, after listening to you, it feels as though I have loved too much, yet I haven't in this life. I have been on my own for years."

"Your feelings belong to that past lifetime where you had a lot of experiences with sex and love. This is why you knew at a young age, in this life, that sex was not love. Some relationships are beneficial; others can be detrimental. Once a link has been made with a soul mate, a structure is created. Your attachment with this past man as your stepfather was never meant to be sexual—neither was your friendship with him in this life. Nevertheless, it served the purpose of releasing the pain from that life, for in this life it was acceptable. This structure will now start dissolving; you may find yourself going down. Don't fight this; it's part of the emotional release. There are many levels of love. When soul has fulfilled itself, the love is meant to disperse; however, it doesn't if people don't let go. Understanding the bigger picture helps this process and leaves no room for regrets or blame. This is what is happening to the remaining energy between you—it is being transmuted. Your love for him is in the process of becoming eternal, and then it will have a future in another dimension where sex, pain, and possessiveness don't belong. Be at peace with your past friendship—it has been fulfilled. As you adjust to the freedom of a clearer emotional body, your feelings of attraction for him will completely disappear. It is part of your journey toward freedom."

She then left. As I sat gazing at the water, suddenly I felt so ordinary, so human. It was hard to conceive of her visit, yet I had all the words written down. Driving home, I decided to make a nice dinner. A friend was coming round, and I called in at the local wine shop for a bottle of red wine. As I was walking out, I heard a voice call out my name. I turned around. It was Deane. We both said hi and continued walking; there was now a distinct barrier of detached energy between us. This natural detachment made it hard to envisage a past with him; the love between us had certainly changed its level. That night as I lay in bed, reflecting on the day, Lalesha arrived again.

"This attachment has now been cleared. Attachments are held in by thoughts and feelings. Alignment of your thoughts and feelings—not suppression of them—needs to happen; we will speak about 'thoughts' tomorrow. A congested emotional body builds toxins in the physical body. You are about to release much. Sleep, and out of your body you will be taken to a place where past lives are transmuted. You are now on the road toward cleansing your past lives; indulge yourself in this experience."

Lalesha had asked me to become a child again. I did feel like a child tonight, a very tired one. I needed rest, and sleep was most desirable. As I was tucking myself in, my young daughter arrived by my bedside.

"Take teddy, Mummy. He will keep you company tonight."

This made me even more emotional; as Celeste had no idea what I had written down. She was only nine, yet she was so in tune with what I was going through—maybe she was there? At this point, I realised my attachment with her soul was most definitely special, and I had to carefully see her through into adulthood without disturbing the delicate psychic ability she was showing signs of having.

Chapter 20

My Astral Body

Stirring from a deep sleep, I became aware that I could smell the new man I had met six months ago. Cliff lived in another city a long distance from me. We had met six times; the last time I had spent the night with him. His warm, attractive scent was permeating the bedroom. Opening my eyes, I looked around to see if he was beside me. He wasn't; I was alone in my own bed. Then I realised—how could I smell him when the flu had progressed to an almighty cold? I couldn't even smell my own food. Turning over in bed, I wrapped the covers around me. It was cold; I didn't want to face another day of children and housework. I would rather stay in bed imbibing his smell, sensing this feeling. The world within me was more comforting than the physical world around me. I lay for awhile within the bliss of dreaming, abruptly broken by children's yells.

"Mummy, we'll be late for school!" my younger daughter cried.

"Mummy, what can we have for lunch today?" my younger son called.

Two sets of eyes were looking at me. "Mum, you haven't had your walk; get up and have your walk," he continued.

My routine of walking before breakfast was a pattern my children had adapted to. This was my way of tuning into the day ahead. My son's ten-year-old green eyes were looking at me with strength, like a guide. Celeste took control and started to make the lunches. When young children show this type of concern, love is generated. Motherhood kicked in. I jumped out of bed.

I drove them to school safely and then returned to do my housework. The house felt empty, devoid of energy. My past was becoming a ghost. Mentally I went blank, so I decided to go to the gym again to dry out this heavy cold in the sauna. When I arrived, my body felt better so I decided to exercise. Today the people and the exercise machines didn't look a blur at all; everything appeared clear. My memory of Dean had disappeared. As I started on the rowing machine, I reflected on Cliff. He had done rowing as a sport years before I had met him. A man at the gym walked past me smelling of stale perspiration. I jumped, remembering what Lalesha had told me. Far out! A life as a prostitute where I liked the smell of perspiration—yuck! I transferred my thoughts back to the nice smell I had experienced upon waking. I started rowing faster. I wanted to see him.

Why can't life move faster? I questioned, pushing myself as fast as I could go. The adrenaline started pumping; the gym assistant walked past, observed the speed I was doing, then questioningly looked at me. I acknowledged her concern by saying my flu was almost better; not really true, but how could she know what was going on within me? I didn't even know. A clash between my body and senses had begun. Frustration was starting to build. I made it to the sauna, and I asked Lalesha to help me calm down.

"You must wait until tonight," she replied.

"Can you not give me one piece of information over Cliff?" I pleaded.

"Not until you return home. You must learn to contain yourself."

I couldn't agree. I didn't feel I should have to wait, so I drove to the same water's edge where yesterday she couldn't stop talking, then tried again. Nothing! She had withdrawn. I waited another hour, trying to force contact. I did not wish to pick up my children from school while in this unhappy state. Lalesha still wouldn't reply.

I kept telepathically asking her questions. *Why can't I meet a man that lives in the same town? Why so far away? Why is it so slow? Is this relationship just a light in the dark to remove me from my past suffering?* Unanswered, I drove home, collecting the children from school while feeling like a robot.

And that's another point, Lalesha—I threw the words at the ethers. *This man makes robots. How can a man who makes robots understand me?* I could hear her laugh but still no words were coming forth.

Arriving home, the noise from the children seemed amplified. I knew leaving the door open for Lalesha was making me more sensitive. *That is why the sooner you talk to me, the better,* I yelled out telepathically. No answer! Well, one thing her withdrawal did prove to me was that I couldn't make up her words; therefore her reality as a spirit guide overlooking my life was real! By the time I had put the children to bed, tiredness had calmed me down. Too exhausted to try to write, I went to sleep.

Waking in the night, still experiencing a yearning for Cliff, I lay in bed wondering why I was so focused on having a man beside me. It was so embarrassing; I had never felt like that before. What had caused this desperate attitude? Then I spotted it. It was the Christmas before my mother died. I had been waiting for the children to go to sleep so I could wrap their presents. Celeste got out of bed, came straight up to me, and said, "Mummy, I don't want any presents. I want a new father for Christmas." These words hit me in the heart, and that was when I decided to move forward and once again find love. Before that, I had been too busy being a solo mother to even consider it.

Lalesha finally arrived. She said, "Celeste will be all right; children build a new emotional body with each new incarnation. Every time you are happy, her emotions lift. Not having a father is not the issue; it's the quality time you share with her. Many children grow up with one parent, and they are fine. It is normal and natural for children to yearn for love and want a father and mother. However, with this new generation, love between parents is going through a process of refinement. Without spiritual understanding, it's almost impossible for relationships to survive. Yearning for love, because of loneliness, can force a person's emotions to go backwards to the last time they shared love. This causes a lot of people to return to a previous relationship, but without the lessons involved in their breakup being learned, more confusion is created. Sentimental thoughts and feelings are the greatest blocks to the future, as they prevent change."

"Yes, Lalesha, I believe you, but I can't work this connection out. If I let go of him, he rings—has he actually become my past, like Deane?"

She replied, "Do you feel you are moving into the future?"

"No. For some reason, I don't."

"Then you are not on the right track."

"How do I get back on track?"

"You need to understand your thoughts as well as your feelings. We see your thoughts manifesting as a body. We call this the astral body, the body of communication, the original motivator of telepathy. Your astral body is a body of lighter energy that you travel in. Whenever you think of another person, this astral body of yours travels to them. It was designed to work as a communicator between your destiny links and your physical life. When somebody thinks of you, they are 'right there' beside you in their astral body. This is what happened yesterday morning when you could smell him; he was travelling to you by thinking of you with love. You returned his love by thinking about him. The astral body does have an aroma—the higher the love, the stronger the scent.

"Both of you felt a boost of energy from this astral communication, but as the day wore on, both of you were confronted with your past and present difficulties, including the physical distance between you both. When the 'destiny time' comes, you will both have a choice to make an effort to see each other and move forward or allow the past to block the flow of new love. The time is not now."

"What if I move forward—and he doesn't?"

"Then you would be the one to fulfil your destiny. You are entering a new dimension of understanding. Destiny rarely waits for an attachment to catch up. If you work on your own life—and you are ready for your new cycle—it happens.

"You need to understand your thoughts more. Wherever your thoughts are, you are in your astral body. This is what your astral body is for—to communicate your desires. Your thoughts (desires) need to be in alignment with your destiny, not opposing it. Unwind, and tomorrow concentrate on the physical plane. Be aware of your thoughts; discipline them into alignment by living in the moment. This will bring you right down to the earth plane and give your astral body a healing. Don't become melancholy, know this to be an in-between time before you find the correct thoughts for your earthly future. Try hard to focus on what you are doing and lose yourself in physical activities. As soon as you are ready, we will talk about your new destiny cycle. When you understand this, you will not be concerned about whether he moves forward or not. It will make no difference to your future."

I realised that whatever I thought or felt was going to have an impact on my future. I had to get it right. This part of my journey was beginning to feel unstable. I did not know if Cliff would be there for me or not, but what worried me the most was my thoughts and feelings. I didn't want them to interfere with the plan of my new cycle. I went back to sleep, asking Lalesha to prepare me in the night to be clear enough to understand my future.

Again I was awakened out of sleep. This time Nannette arrived beside me.

"Nannette, you look so beautiful and so young."

"That is because I am in my light body—so is Lalesha. You have a light body; everybody does. It is as close as you can get to your spirit, and you don't lose this body of light when you incarnate into a physical body. You are just at a distance from it."

"How far away is mine?"

"At times, very close. This is what I came to talk to you about. Lalesha is one of the new spirit guides for the Aquarian Age. She has understanding over how to integrate all higher bodies with the physical body and how to recharge one's physical life.

"How many bodies do we have?"

"First you have your spirit, which can be referred to as your light body; this is the body your spirit travels in. When you incarnate into an earth body, your spirit enters the slightly slower pale blue dimension of soul, for the vibration of earth, which is even slower still, can't sustain the fast frequency from your spirit. This is why your spirit takes on clothes of soul, and this is in the form of a pale blue garment of light. From there, your soul travels to a dimension filled with white light where you are given a higher self body. This is the body that can guide and protect your soul; if you contact your higher self, it can correct what has gone wrong with your destiny. You can also know what karma you are carrying and the lessons you need to learn by tuning in to your higher self. You can contact your higher self by visualising white light; Lalesha will teach you how to do this tomorrow. Right now we are explaining your astral body.

"When you take on a new earth life, an astral body has to be created to give your mind the ability to expand. If your mind was locked in flesh and bone, it wouldn't get far—would it? A new emotional body is also formed so that your feelings have expression, and this starts being created after you are born. This new astral and emotional body is formed from the thoughts and feelings you experience from the surrounding environment you grow up in—coupled with the emanations from your soul. A person who incarnates into a harmonious situation easily obtains flows from their soul. It is harder for those that don't have this privilege. Prior to being born, your soul travels to your future parent or parents. Sometimes an incarnating soul will remain attached to a future mother years before conception; other times, it happens at the moment of conception. Incarnating into an earth life is not a simple venture. For example, an evolved soul would be looking at their future parents' karma; they would look at the genetics and sort out what DNA they wanted from either parent. They would choose the best astrological time for conception to take place before connecting; knowing that all this energy would set the stage for what they wanted to do in their new life. You chose parents that you had no karma with; because they didn't belong to any organised religion, you grew up without indoctrination. This enabled you to receive psychic flows easily. Because of this, you didn't question what you could see or hear. You accepted it as normal."

"Nannette, I did. It has often crossed my mind why my parents never said anything. During dinners, I would often say what was going to happen in the future. If I said when one of the older members in the family was going to die, it usually came to pass—but they just kept eating. I still find this unusual."

"Their souls were aware of what you would do in this life, and this inner knowing stopped their human selves from reacting. Your incarnation was guided before you connected. What you are doing now is relearning what your soul already knows. Your human self is catching up to your true level; this experience is helping your soul to grow. The levels are the same for all of humanity. The way people learn is different; this is what makes people individuals. You are sharing your individual journey, but the lessons you are going through all people will experience—not in the same way, in their own way—so you will feel lonely at times. Don't let this loneliness stop you from moving. Start loving the lessons involved in living life. Acknowledge people's dark sides. Know it is only the dark before the dawn; when they overcome their lessons you will share a love that surpasses understanding. You don't need to put yourself in others' shoes anymore; you just need to acknowledge that they are here to learn, like you.

"Go back to sleep, you have a big day with Lalesha tomorrow, and your mind needs a rest. She has explained how your mind can be referred to as your astral body and how every time you think, it becomes active. It is also the body you travel in when you go to sleep at night, but if you keep thinking about your earth life, you will only travel within the auric field of earth. To fly higher into the realms of light and love where problems are solved, you need to raise your thoughts to a higher level. There are many astral levels; your astral body is created from your thoughts as a human being and your soul's level of advancement. This combined light energy creates the form that you can call your astral body. It looks similar to your earth body, but it is made out of a stronger fibre so it lasts longer. It also has no lines and no wear or tear."

I was too tired to count all the bodies Lalesha and Nannette were talking about. I went back to sleep, imagining what my astral body looked like. I didn't like how I physically looked; my eyes were sad. Nannette and Lalesha had not been able to remove this from me. Maybe my out of body experiences tonight would shine more light on where I was on my journey.

Chapter 21

My Higher Self

The sun streamed through my bedroom window, waking me from a glorious sleep. I couldn't remember where I had been in my astral body, but something had changed. I felt inspired. I wanted more information, but Lalesha had told me to concentrate on the physical plane. I cleaned the house effortlessly, continuing on to the gym after dropping the children off at school.

Starting on the rowing machine, I closed my eyes, wondering if I could see a picture to explain the elated feeling I had awakened with. With my eyes still closed, I could see a picture of Cliff surrounded in white light looking at me. This picture stayed for about five minutes before merging with the white light around him. As soon as I relaxed in the sauna, Lalesha started with what turned into a very long discourse. So much for concentrating on the physical plane!

"You were looking at his higher self earlier," she said. "Everyone has a higher self, but not many people fully understand this part of their higher consciousness. The higher self guides and energises the mind and then waits for the human self to respond by following its guidance. It is the key part of one's spiritual makeup that corrects destiny when it goes wrong. His higher self was communicating with you, but this doesn't mean the human him is aware of what took place. To help this situation and to avoid disappointment and frustration, you must ask your own higher self to align your thoughts (astral body) with your destiny. The energy is good for us to communicate today. You can go home, and I will explain more about destiny to you. Remember to keep being the child or you will overlap my words with your own wisdom. Because you are a medium, this can easily happen. I don't want anything to interfere with my words."

Eager to hear her clear words and starting to like the attention, I dressed myself and went home. Sitting comfortably in my favourite chair, I had to admit I was sad. Cliff had spoken of meeting up with me for a weekend—and he had promised to ring—yet weeks had gone by without a call. I couldn't ignore the picture I had seen of him. Lalesha had called it his higher self. I had communicated with many people's higher selves. I wanted to communicate with this man's human self—and start a new cycle of destiny in my human, physical life. His higher self communicating with me could mean anything. He could be having another relationship, putting me on hold until he'd worked it through! This thought gave me more sadness. I wanted to use my own psychic, yet what Lalesha had said about interfering made sense. The logical thing to do would be to give him a ring and suggest meeting up, but then I would have to fit into his schedule. Something inside me didn't feel like bothering. As soon as I thought this, Lalesha returned.

"Lalesha, can you tell me where I am with this relationship?"

"You are trying to understand your destiny."

"Isn't he my destiny?"

"Not necessarily, I will explain. True destiny is a flow of energy that responds to your soul's calling. You are in the process of obtaining another level of your soul's journey. This will bring about a change with your thinking, making your needs different to what they are now. This is what you are going through. Until this change of attitude occurs, destiny stands back. One door must fully close before another opens. You are moving out of the hands of fate into the arms of destiny; you are changing from being a victim to taking control of your life. To be in control, one must understand the difference between fate and destiny.

"Destiny is a thread of divine energy containing situations in life that not only agree with your human dreams but also make your soul delight in anticipation of the experience. Fate occurs when one has gone off their true destiny road; when this happens, fate comes in to correct their life. Fate is more on the level of lessons; destiny is more to do with soul expression. At present, your life is a mixture of fate and destiny. You are not free to love yet. If your destiny came in now, because you are a combination of the past you and the new you, you wouldn't be clear enough to see it. I am not asking you to live on faith; I am asking you to raise yourself into the frequency of your higher self, for this part of your higher consciousness knows your true destiny and can point you in the right direction. The easiest way to connect is to visualise white light circulating in the centre of your forehead. Remain focused on the white light for as long as you can; when you feel you have absorbed some, let it go and continue living your physical life. It will start its passage toward connecting with your mind with guidance. Visualising white light is the place you go when you need direction from your higher self. You don't always need to receive this guidance in the form of words to know you have connected. After visualising the white light, your higher self will confirm you have connected by giving you a burst of positive energy. This is the sign you look for. Receiving energy from your higher self is what's important. It relies on visualising white light, and it works like a magnet, drawing it closer to you.

"Running around and working in with this man's schedule is the old way—it won't work anymore. It goes back to your mother's time when men did all the leading. There have been big changes with male and female energy; most women won't tolerate the old ways of a male-dominated society. However, many are trying to fight this by doing better than men. This is another form of dominance that leads to conflict. Women would be better off to acknowledge the male energy, then acknowledge the power of their own feminine energy—see it as equal and learn to share, not compete. You cannot gain power by taking another's power. This is a basic truth. Females are not going to gain power by taking away males' power. Equality of the sexes—men and women—heavily relies on women becoming equal by their actions toward men and vice versa.

"You can change your feeling of insecurity by changing your vibration. Reach up and feel the cool, calm confidence of your higher self. This is the part that can guide you through this time. Don't work in with his schedule—work in with the schedule of your own higher self. It knows. This is why his higher self travelled to you today; it was trying to inform you of his unavailability at present. Practise aligning yourself with your own higher self before you make any decisions over what to do. Guides are not permitted to tell you what to do if it is going to interfere with a lesson you are learning, but your higher self has this right.

"Your journey at this time is removing any attachments that are unworthy of your soul. Don't judge others who are stuck in relationships that aren't working. This transition from Piscean to Aquarian energy is affecting people; many relationships will break up during this time as the new energy is geared toward soul fulfilment. If one is not in touch with the soul, life will be unstable, and they will become discontented. The benefit from linking with your higher self is that it enables you to reach the destiny your soul wants; this alone gives stability. Until you get there, keep writing down all your thoughts and feelings. Observe how you are changing; this will confirm that what you are experiencing is not fantasy. As I explained before, you are clearing the way for a better human life by achieving a higher level of destiny.

"Destiny has many levels; if you wish to obtain your new level, you must remain connected to your higher self. As a destiny spirit guide, my purpose is to bring about happenings that are compatible with a person's soul. They are not so much human desires—unless they are in agreement with the soul."

"Does agreement between the soul and human self happen often, Lalesha?"

"Yes, but it happens rarely. In the future, it will be considered essential; a person will not wish to make a decision without the consent of their soul."

"I'm getting confused, Lalesha. Didn't you say I needed guidance from my higher self—and now you are saying I need consent from my soul? I always thought my higher consciousness was my higher self."

"Guidance from your soul can happen via your higher self—that's what it's there for. It can be confusing to understand your different bodies, but it is worth clarifying.

Very rarely does one's soul speak; as I said earlier, the door to the soul is through the heart. When you experience soul, it is more to do with feelings, sometimes intense feelings. There is a distinct difference between human desires and desires from the soul; your higher self is the part that sees both and can help you clearly see what your soul wants you to do. Higher consciousness is pure spiritual energy that surrounds all the bodies; and, you could say, they are all made from this energy. On your journey of soul fulfilment at present, one aspect of yourself is moving toward freedom from past lives. With somebody else, it could be fulfilment of a productive business deal. The soul is concerned with expanding itself, and it chooses human events to do this. As your higher self has more input in your life your feelings will change dramatically."

"Well, Lalesha, if this happens to me, and I meet up with Cliff again, he could feel like a stranger—if I'm still changing."

She laughed, "Or you could feel in love. Yes, dear one, this is a big problem. I observe many who fall in love. As they mentally and emotionally change, they move apart and become strangers to each other."

"Don't you find this sad?"

"No, dear one, I do not. The reason being, if two people separate, it means the soul can no longer progress through that situation or relationship. All people are alive on this planet to express their souls. If you were created to concentrate solely on your physical life, your body would continue to live. It would not die. This is a temporary existence for your physical body. Don't overlook this special time to go within and know your own soul's personality."

"Does soul have a personality?"

"Yes, and when you blend with it, you become a powerful personality."

"Lalesha, the more I write down these words from you, an intense yearning to feel and share love stirs within me."

"Dear one, you are starting to feel your own soul. On another level, it is already linked to others. However, you cannot possess another's soul—you can only own yours. Love your soul by honouring or acknowledging that you have a created destiny. People don't understand destiny energy; they usually want it to have an inflated balloon of luxuries. Sometimes it does, but destiny can be the end of one's life at fifty-four—like Nannette. However sad losing a loved one can be, when you become aware of the multidimensional self (higher bodies) relocating on the Other Side becomes as real as emigrating to another country. It is all part of one's soul journey. Get to know your own soul more, and you will be free to lovingly share. You have removed many layers; your soul is already starting to shine through. Remember, destiny only comes into being as a structure to support the soul. I would say you are not waiting for destiny; destiny is waiting for you to catch up. You have been conditioned about how you should feel about yourself and others; we are getting rid of any conditioning."

"Lalesha, I have accepted that I'm different. I don't really care what people think about me."

"Oh, yes, you do! When it comes to being a mother, you try to fit in and follow modern ways of helping your younger children grow. This blocks the intuitive ability you have to allow your children to flow with the light from their own souls. All your children have a connection with their soul light. You are very blessed."

"You are really making me face myself, Lalesha. I felt I was an individual because I try my best in this world where people do behave like robots, all saying the same hellos and good-byes. I have never liked fitting into the mould."

"Neither have your children. In the future, they will all follow creative pathways. Given time, they will fulfil much."

"I love their creativity, Lalesha."

"Yes, but lately, when your older children visit, their financial situations are the first thing you question. If they were to ignore their creative flows and concentrate on earning money for the sake of a bigger bank balance, their souls would starve. This is why those that have enormous wealth are usually the unhappiest people on this planet. When people put all their energy into acquiring possessions, without acknowledging the reality that possessions cannot go with them, separation from their soul starts occurring. Of course, one needs money to survive, but the world is in chaos; survival mode is where most are. This isn't all karmic; it's the state of the world. Awareness of the continuing journey of the soul will usher in a new love of material equality for humanity. People will wish wholeheartedly to give and to share. Conditioning over materiality is in the process of being broken down; this is why money is so unstable. The more you have, the more you need. It is a never-ending cycle. A balance will occur on the planet in the future, and people will not starve."

"Lalesha, I didn't realise I had taken on this old-fashioned attitude. When will it go?"

"You are in the process of it right now. You are creating a new cycle through understanding your different bodies. Today you learned about your higher self and the impact it can have on your soul and your destiny. At present, you have one foot in the past and one foot in the future. If you can love yourself enough, you will release your grip on the past. The past will become a blank, not the future, for you will be clear enough to carve a new pathway."

"I want to Lalesha, but every time I come close, I feel as if I am travelling away from the earth's atmosphere into the deep blue universe. To be honest, I am frightened; part of me feels I am dying. And I can't—I have responsibilities as a solo mother."

I could see Lalesha smiling; she moved closer to me. "This is the time to trust; the old you is truly dying. The night sky pulsates with activity; it is calling you. Follow it. Tomorrow, when you have freed yourself up by digesting this, I will speak more about your soul. It truly does have a future that you are almost ready to believe in."

Then she left. What a mouthful! My mind was still set on having a day off by concentrating on the physical plane as she had told me to. Maybe this had changed because the energy for communicating was good. Whatever the reason, I was determined to experience the physical plane. It was time to pick the children up; I grabbed our swimsuits, and we went to the hot pools. It felt lovely. They didn't want to get out, but when I promised them fish and chips, they jumped out in a hurry. We drove to the fresh fish market and enjoyed a tasty early dinner. The natural minerals in the hot pools had made them sleepy; they both climbed into bed two hours earlier than normal. Wonderful! Now I could digest what Lalesha had said.

Today I had woken up still connected to my astral body; tomorrow I hoped to wake up connected to my higher self, as this seemed to be the key toward achieving my new cycle. I went to sleep with the curtains open so I could view the starry night sky. All the spiritual activity around me was replacing my fear with a new love of the unknown.

Chapter 22

Soul Mates

I awoke on Tuesday morning with a sense of organisation. I felt connected to my higher self, but I visualised white light—just to make sure. The burst of positive energy I felt confirmed that I was connected.

I was excited about the knowledge Lalesha would give me, but I had six readings to do before I could communicate with her. I didn't want to do them; my mind was more interested in her viewpoint on soul than on other people's problems. The flow was there for writing. I could feel it; maybe my work as a medium was my old cycle, and my life as a writer was my new future. This thought seemed to take me somewhere. I started to dream off until my first client arrived. Faye was always so grateful for any information I gave; it was so easy to do a reading for her. Out of all my regular clients, her love life was extremely colourful. My life was like a nun's in comparison to hers; today she was wearing bright orange boots, blue jeans, a turquoise scarf, and purple jacket. Even in loud colours, she looked amazing. I was always in black; I couldn't wear much colour because it would detract from the coloured lights I could see in my mind.

"Hi darlin'," she called out as she entered my house.

Her voice was also very loud; she sounded like a singer. I started dreaming off, imagining her as a singer in a past life.

"Watcha seein', darlin'?"

I pulled myself back and started tuning in. Interestingly enough, she had been a singer. The man she was seeing at present had been her manager in that life; as soon as I started telling her this, she started crying. She always did this; the tiniest piece of truth would get a big reaction.

"He is always trying to manage me," she said through her sobs. "I can't stand it; it is hurting my soul."

She wouldn't stop crying. I decided to tell her what Lalesha had been teaching me about the emotional body. "Your emotional body is full from your past experiences, including your past lives. You are releasing some of this pain while you cry. You can't harm your soul because your emotional body acts as a shock absorber to protect it. It is your emotional body you need to clear."

She stopped crying and said, "But sometimes there's nothing in my life to account for how I feel; frustrations build up when people start organising me. When I analyse what they're saying, it's not that demanding, but I can't work it out."

Faye was so open and honest; at that stage, I gave over and channelled my spirit guide. The message took her back into that life—and beyond into a life where she had not only organised but dominated those close to her. The lesson she was learning this lifetime was to allow others to be themselves; by doing this, she would remove the karma she was carrying. This was a revelation to Faye. She was very soft and loving to others, but she admitted to always having afterthoughts about them. She would conclude her thoughts with what she thought they should do—and they would usually end up doing it. Unconsciously, the power of her thoughts was organising others.

"Thanks, darlin'. I'm off to study my thoughts."

Impulsively I answered, "Align them with your higher self. Just visualise white light circulating in the centre of your forehead every time you find yourself creating a scenario for others, and it will guide you toward thinking differently."

Half an hour went by as we discussed the benefit of connecting with one's higher self. By the time I had finished client number six, I was exhausted. The last two were friends, so I allowed them more time even though it drained me. Going over the day, I wondered if their problems were making me tired. That was when I realised that their self-centredness was affecting me. It was difficult to get them to face themselves; someone else was always to blame. Love usually came in after I'd finished a day of readings, but all I could feel was sick in my stomach. Remembering what Lalesha had said to Faye about karma, and just in case I was feeling mine, I powerfully visualised white light. Slowly warmth entered my head and body, changing my frequency. I started to communicate with Lalesha.

"You are on the brink of obtaining clarity," she said. "This means you will start to discern, with logic, the reality of others' situations. You will lose your dreamy, loving nature that concentrates on the good in others. The clearer you become, the more able you will be to see the cause of their problems and the dramas they create to avoid looking at what they are here to learn. Your soul doesn't need to experience their blocks; you are not always aware of what your loving, dreamy nature absorbs from people. This is the part you must change; many friends often take advantage of this dreamy nature of yours—and they end up draining you."

"But I understood true spirituality was relieving life's difficulties by helping others."

"Many think this; however, most help is on a level of propping up people's bad behaviour. It is time for all to wake up and realise what they are living a life for. Logic is needed at this point of your journey. You can't keep giving love to people; you must start referring to their karma."

"Honestly, Lalesha, if I start explaining karma to my clients, I would lose two-thirds of them."

"Yes, you may, because a lot of people give up on spirituality when they reach the time where they have to face themselves and change. Many of them revert to the physical plane for comfort and happiness, turning their backs on spirituality. Unfulfilled, they become cynical. This is when the heart and mind go out of sync."

"I can understand this Lalesha, because it does take a lot of energy to face oneself. If I had to work in town, I don't think I would have the energy."

"Yes, you would. It only takes a moment to analyse and observe what your thoughts and feelings are doing. This traps and prevents one from creating any new karma. Spirit guides always overlook and help people who are facing themselves. Let's start cleaning up the karma on this planet together; karma is blocking everything—especially destiny."

"Lalesha, is karma blocking my relationship with Cliff?"

"A little. He has a battle going on between his mind and soul—his past and future. Leave him to work it out. Stop thinking of him."

"What will win—his mind or soul?"

"What the soul needs to progress, it eventually gets. But first I will give you more understanding about soul:

"Beyond the veil—behind the consciousness of human living—there is an immense spectrum of oscillating activity exposing itself as blue light. It is huge and contains the soul blueprint of all people living on the planet. Not one fragment of genuine loving expression occurs on this planet without the soul's knowledge and supervision. However, not many people are linked enough with their soul to allow this blueprint to manifest. Most people live their lives from their genetic imprints. Life should follow one's soul blueprint—not the inherited mindsets."

"Have I been living my blueprint?"

"You have fulfilled some of your soul's blueprint, but you still have a lot more to fulfil. At the moment, it is blocked. This is why you need more clarity. There are two distinct centres where you can gain energy to live life. One is by going within and listening to your inner self. This gives you the energy that is right for you. The other centre is mainly functioning by what is considered right or normal by society. This centre is governed by rights and wrongs—judgement; and when one lives their life solely from this viewpoint their soul can't have an input and their blueprint can't manifest."

"Well, Lalesha, no wonder people have difficulty finding a soul mate. If their own soul isn't present, they wouldn't be able to see a person clearly. The attraction would be all physical."

Lalesha smiled, "Yes. The greatest relationships are those that are mentally in tune, have a physical attraction for each other and, most of all, a soul link. When all three are flowing, the love is enormous. It emanates and helps others.

This world needs more love. That is how the blueprint of its future can manifest. It will get there; many advanced souls have love for humanity and are incarnating to help. These souls usually focus more on what they are doing to help humanity than on their own love lives. You could call them workaholics. Most of them link up with an original soul mate and, with their natural understanding of each other, together they bring about change."

"I can identify with that Lalesha. I'm not happy looking at my love life. I'd rather be channelling information to help the planet."

"The first step toward helping the planet is to clear one's own life. Why do you think I am helping you? For once you clear your life you will be able to reach your potential. Soul love truly is powerful. When it comes to personal love, all souls have three original soul mates. This occurs because when spirit descends into soul matter, it splits into three versions of itself; each version has a male and female aspect. All three (or six) are the same soul; these are your original soul mates. There are other souls you can spend lifetimes loving or sharing with. This builds up a rapport, and these souls can be referred to as soul mates—but not original soul mates. Original soul mates have the same purpose. If you could view your blueprint, you would see yourself entwined with one of your original soul mates."

"Lalesha, many search for this type of love."

"Yes, and many never find it. Soul mates connect when both are ready for a new level of love. It is my responsibility to get you to the level where you are free enough to love. That is when what you do will be your own soul choice. Remember the night you met Cliff?"

"Yes."

"Something changed within you. Remember?"

"Oh, yes I do! I was getting ready to go to the first day of the Tauranga Jazz Festival with my son. He's a jazz pianist. As I was having my shower, he called out, 'Hurry up, Mum. I wouldn't want to be your husband'. He'd said it jokingly, but this triggered my lack. I started feeling the emptiness in my heart—and then I became angry. I had experienced enough pain over men. I must have called out to God—and then I spun out somewhere. When I came back, it was like I had lost a few moments in time. But I was peaceful, almost disconnected from my suffering. I knew my energy had changed. Can you elaborate on this experience?"

"Dear one, your nervous system had taken on too much emotional trauma. Your aura short-circuited. In a split-second, you travelled to the soul plane and back. There you absorbed your future, giving you the peace that returned with you."

"Why do I not have that peace with me now?"

"You have used it all up. You need to travel to the soul plane tonight to obtain some more energy from your blueprint. You can do this by asking a spirit guide to transport you there. Give over tonight; ask for help to free yourself of any blocks that are standing in the way of your blueprint. Your stress over Cliff is founded upon not wanting another failed relationship. Unconsciously you have been trying to test him—and me. You are looking for signs. He is one of your original soul mates, and this is why your feelings for him run deep. However, there is one way to find out if he will be there for you in the future—and this is to become the new you with more of your blueprint present in your aura. Your blueprint contains your future. Your level is still changing; it does take time. At present, you are stalemated because of the uncertainty surrounding your relationship with him. This must go through a process of clearing before you are free to love. If he can't meet up, you must let him go."

"This type of love isn't guaranteed?"

"In a way it is because, once a connection has been made with an original soul mate, the process of clearing never ceases. You are kept on your toes. The flame of eternal love will keep you moving toward each other; even if it takes another incarnation to fulfil the love, it will happen. If one soul mate is free and the other isn't, then another of the three original soul mates moves forward and fills the gap. Your blueprint has this knowledge. If a person only has one soul mate present on this earth, and that mate departs the earth life and returns to the afterlife, it is not unusual for the one left behind not to feel lonely because their love can ignite on another level. This is how some people exist without their soul partner beside them. It is playing out its expression on another dimension; therefore fulfilment is still felt. I am allowed to say you have two original soul mates present on this earth; if this one fails, you will have the choice of another."

"Thank you, Lalesha. That gives me freedom to let go. Many people ask me if the person they have met is their true soul mate. Is there a key to knowing?"

"Yes, when two soul mates connect, their energy has the same frequency. But understanding each other isn't always easy because every soul builds a different structure around them as they journey through their different incarnations. You can always tell a true soul mate by the enormous peace that is generated when they meet.

"It has been a long journey for all of mankind. People are tired, giving up on love—yet it is part of the plan of soul destiny. The more people go within and find their own souls before sharing with others, the faster the process of finding real love will be. You can wait to love another honestly with a soul flow or use another to obtain love at times of need. One way will build you up—and the other will drain you. Love will not be misused.

"Tonight, as you go to sleep, remember to ask to be taken to the soul plane. There we will gently renew you with some more of your blueprint. When you wake up, the feeling from this change of energy will be present in your aura, making you more sensitive. If you honour this by following your heightened intuition, you will work through the last lap faster. You will also help the planet because spiritual energy is powerful; it emanates and affects others. Visualise lots of white light; this will help you remain clear and focused. When you interact with others, look for the threads of destiny behind the karma they are carrying. No matter how ignored destiny is, it still remains in a person's aura. The unfulfilment you see with people usually indicates that karma is blocking the flow of their destiny. There are specialised spirit guides that can remove karma; all people have to do is be willing to face themselves. You have faced yourself enough today; while you sleep, these special guides will remove some more of your karma. You are motoring through it now; tomorrow will be another different day."

It is interesting how Lalesha slipped in that I was working through karma. I was relieved that she didn't elaborate on it because I felt I'd been given as much as I could handle. I guess she didn't need to because the energy I used to face myself created the perfect environment for karma to automatically be released. She had helped me believe I could obtain peace—not by not getting angry and spinning out, but by asking to be taken to the soul plane. Once again, she had created a shift in my consciousness. If Cliff couldn't make it to be with me, I knew the peace her knowledge was giving me would replace any gap in my heart.

Chapter 23

Clearing a Past Life

Expecting to wake up clear after last night's excursion with Lalesha, I was disappointed. I felt let down. I had done what she had said by asking to be taken to the soul plane to absorb some of my blueprint. This was the result—I felt terrible. Looking around my messy bedroom, I decided I'd had enough of writing—and not enough reality.

Reality! What is that? A house you can no longer pay the mortgage on.

I was depressed. I didn't want any more wisdom from a spirit guide. Dragging myself from my bed, I made coffee and sat down to work it all out logically. Suddenly a shattering occurred in my emotional body—similar to what I experienced when relationships ended. I needed the guide's wisdom! She was helping me, and I needed this help now! I tried to remove my sad feelings by visualizing white light. This helped me focus, but the awful feeling wouldn't go. I wondered if, with the spirit guide's adjustment of my blueprint during the night, my relationship with Cliff had ended before it had really begun. When I remembered how Lalesha had told me not to think of him, I pushed any thoughts of him out of my mind. This did not remove the impulse to cry. My eldest son had stayed on for a few days after the jazz festival and had just left to take his younger brother and sister to school. I took advantage of the free time and forced myself off to the gym, hoping it would help in the alignment process Lalesha was talking about.

As I started on the rower, I noticed my speed was becoming faster without trying. *My body is progressing—even though the rest of me doesn't feel it has.* In fact, compared to the heightened feeling I had experienced last week, it appeared that I had gone backwards spiritually and forwards physically. I closed my eyes, while rowing, hoping my mind would align with my body. A picture of a young woman appeared in my consciousness. She had long, golden-brown hair, a slim body, olive skin, and huge green eyes. As I observed and concentrated on this picture, the shattered sadness inside of me removed itself from my body into her eyes. I kept concentrating—and then I realised she was me! Not now, not in this life. I knew this was a past experience of mine from another life. Why was it there? I hurried through the exercises so I could sit down in the sauna and ask Lalesha. But the sauna was full of women. In my receptive state, their voices sounded like fishwives. So I dressed and left.

My intuition had been heightened. I could sense Lalesha wasn't available to communicate with me, so I called in to ask a friend to lunch. The café was buzzing with people conversing. I looked around for signs of any destiny energy in their eyes. Three people stared back at me as if I was prying; I felt uncomfortable and wanted to leave. Acknowledging that this was a cycle I had to go through alone, I said good-bye to my friend and returned home.

Intermittently, emotional pain and calmness were interacting with my feelings—I was experiencing pain and peace simultaneously. The rest of the day passed routinely, but these opposing feelings would not go away. That night as I was cleaning my teeth, I glanced in the mirror, I felt so different. I guess I was checking to see if my face still looked the same. Gradually my aura started to appear. I had been taught to see auras by staring into the mirror, focusing on one spot around the temple area, and then the aura would appear. I was doing this unconsciously—gazing at the colours while considering, that even though Lalesha had not communicated today, it had been constructive. The young woman I had seen in my mind, at the gym, impressed herself over my entire face. I could still feel my own mind, but her presence was layered over my feelings. Taking control, I finished brushing my teeth and washed my face. Her presence was so strong that I could feel her different bone structure as I dried my face. I sat down. The house was quiet; the children were asleep. I asked for Lalesha; I wanted to know about this experience.

As she began communicating, I realised I needed to listen carefully.

"This young woman was you in the past life I spoke to you about. I have been waiting for a chance to complete explaining it to you, but you were so enthusiastic over clearing the pain from the past men in your life that you didn't allow me to continue. Now I can finish the story of that lifetime.

"When you escaped to the city to start a new life, you fell in love with the owner of the paper—and he with you. You married, giving birth to two children. Ten years of happiness were fulfilled—until your friend the doctor came to visit. Your new life gave him a sense of joy. He encouraged you all to go out to dinner. The restaurant was packed. Amidst the gaiety of conversation and food, you were unaware that somebody was watching you. As the three of you lifted your glasses up to friendship and happiness, your stepfather, dressed in rags and drunk, lunged forward, spat on you, yelling, "So this is where prostitution has led you!" He then disappeared into the night. The silence of death fell, shattering your life into pieces. You ran out into the night. You passed restaurants, bars, even brothels—re-stimulating your past experiences. You kept running, blind with pain and fear. You stepped off the curb, on a corner, and were killed by an oncoming taxi.

"You arrived on the Other Side in shock; much healing was required to adjust you to this other dimension. Back on earth, your husband and friend consoled themselves. In the morning, the doctor told him of your past as a prostitute. He was shocked as the story of your past was exposed. The soul love you had shared became tainted; this love then returned to the soul plane for a future time. As you sleep tonight, this past life of yours will be transmuted. This means the painful shattering experience residing in your subconscious will be removed completely—and you will be one step further into your new cycle.

"Your journey to the soul plane last night revived this past life shell; now it is the right time for it to be removed. This will happen tonight whilst you sleep. Your awareness has initiated this happening. When you wake up tomorrow, you will feel love in your heart. When a past life is transmuted, it clears the way for more love to be released. If you think of Cliff, you must love him unconditionally. Let go with love and work in with destiny—this is your road to freedom. Keep writing. You are almost there. Soon you will be ready for your new cycle. Don't lose sight of the destination you're aiming toward. You are on a journey to clear any emotional pain from the past, including past lives. I will now give you an affirmation that will help until you stabilise with your new level.

I affirm
I am on a journey of love, my focus is love.
Whatever confronts me on my journey
Melts within my aura of purified love.
The heavenly waters of creation
Daily cleanse my interactions with people
For I no longer blame or judge the
Differing viewpoints of others
Seeing them as on a level of learning.
And it is in the practising of unconditional love
I am freed.
I now fearlessly move forward to my next level
Constantly asking my Higher Self
To align my thoughts with my
Soul's true destiny that awaits me with love.
Therefore I only claim what is mine in this world
And the worlds I visit in my
Developing expansion of consciousness.

Comfortable with the care and love from this spirit guide, I relaxed. I knew the owner of the paper had been Cliff. What the guide was hinting at implied he wouldn't be there for me, but the love circulating in my aura after writing down the affirmation gave me license to drift off to sleep with thoughts of love for him.

Chapter 24

Unconditional Love

Not knowing why, I jumped out of bed ready to conquer the world. That was when I remembered how Lalesha had said I would wake up feeling love. If I thought of Cliff, she told me to love him unconditionally. Maybe I already had because my love for him felt very small in comparison to my own life; it was almost insignificant. I was so energised and ready for action that I repeated the pattern that was helping me through this time: dropping the children off at school and heading straight for the gym.

I flew through the exercises. My aging body was certainly changing. I felt younger. Bounding into the changing rooms, I immersed myself in the purifying water of a shower and covered my hair in conditioner. I was ready to relax in the warmth of the sauna. The day was unseasonably cold. The sauna always made me dream of summer; my muscles would relax in response to the dry heat. The sauna was full of talking women. Today it didn't bother me; my feet were on the ground, and I could join in. All five women were solo mothers; as they recounted pieces of their lives with men, the trauma they'd lived through and were still experiencing started affecting me. Some were so hurt that they never wanted to share love again. I started feeling sorry for myself as I remembered my own negative experiences.

Massaging moisturiser into my forehead, I could feel frown lines. *I bet each line was caused by the stress of a man in my life.*

A tall, slim, blonde woman said, “How many children do you have?”

“Five,” I replied.

“Five! You poor thing.”

“Well, they range from nine to twenty-nine,” I said, feeling a little proud because a song about love was drifting through the sauna. My son was the pianist in the band, and ‘Soul Train’ was fast becoming a hit on the local FM station.

“Twenty-nine!” They all turned and stared at me. “You don’t look that old.”

I was coming up again. Suddenly, I didn’t want any self-pity aimed at me. I took advantage of the song. “Hear that song on the radio? My son’s the pianist; he’s a musician and a really nice man. No abusive, irresponsible, selfish male will ever stop me from loving again. I won’t tolerate it. I’ll change my life and attract a different level of love. This is part of the reason I’m here at the gym. My attitude has changed so much. I want my body to meet up to how I feel.”

“What you’re really saying,” said a rather overweight lady, “is that you’re looking for a man, and you want to look good.” She tightened the towel around her chest. “I personally couldn’t be bothered anymore.”

“Then why are you here?” asked another.

The conversation was becoming heated; each was fuelling the others into hating men again. When they left,

I was left with the negative energy that love doesn't really exist anymore. I stayed for a while, thinking about my own experiences with love. I couldn't hate; ever since Lalesha had explained destiny to me, I knew we created what we needed to progress. What was I creating at present? I had felt a door open for Cliff, but he hadn't entered. Somehow, I could still feel love for him. Was my old, dreamy nature still present? I didn't even have a plan for my future.

"Then you had better get one," interrupted Lalesha.

Surprised she had been listening, I answered, "Without him?"

"Yes," she replied.

This jolted me right out of feeling love. Maybe Lalesha was finally telling me he couldn't make it. I knew I had progressed, but I had learned that destiny can rearrange when the energy shifts. I knew this, but I thought something *had* changed because I had woken up with so much love.

"Don't hold any pictures," she said. "Your thoughts are interfering."

This part of my journey was becoming confusing: *Love him unconditionally? He is a soul mate. Stop thinking of him!* It sounded to me like the guide was on his side. Dropping back down into my human self, I started losing the positive feelings of love I had woken with. Even though my love for him was shrinking, I still didn't have a clear answer about whether he would be in my future or not. I was annoyed by him taking so long to work through the conditioning of his life. *Why do I always have to wait?* I no longer wanted his memory. I wanted action. Original soul mate or not, no one is indispensable. I was giving love to this man, and none was returning. I wanted to break the spell he had over me.

As I headed for the shower, I passed the lady with the long blonde hair. Her hair had changed to a mousy brown.

She put on her glasses and meekly walked away. I knew what I had seen was one of her past lives. *This must be the mesmerism that past life energy generates. Maybe I am in a dream; maybe all the love I've been feeling for Cliff belongs to that other life. Now that it's been cleared, the love's gone!*

Walking out of the gym, my heart felt sad. I went into my mind—and it felt clear. Deciding to only relate to my mind, I started coming up and feeling very good about myself—in fact, very good. This was my journey. I didn't care whether I had lived as a prostitute or a nun—if that's what my soul had needed to experience, I was proud of it. As for Cliff, he could find his own soul. He was a useless, weak man—and I didn't want him.

As soon as I said this forcefully into the atmosphere, Lalesha responded with, "You will wound him on the thought plane. Go home, and we will talk."

Driving home, I realised I was swinging from the depths of no confidence to being powerfully confident. Maybe Lalesha could explain this contrast of feeling. After everything I had been through with her, I was very confused. At home, I once again picked up my pen.

She said, "When you are hurt, you mustn't lash out like this. It will make you hard and drop the level of your astral body. Your thoughts are real to your astral body. When you have harmful thoughts about another person, these thoughts travel and attack their aura. Even though this activity is unseen, they feel it. Maybe he is weak and maybe it's his lesson in this life to overcome that; it's not your place to judge. You need to concentrate on what *you* are doing. All this negative thinking is congesting your astral body. You woke up this morning with a clear astral body. That is why you felt so confident. Don't drop down. Go over what I said about loving him unconditionally. If your emotions still hurt, go quiet, sit with your hurt, absorb it, and allow it to thaw. Your emotional body also went through a healing last night; this is what automatically occurs when some karma is removed. The pain from that past life has now gone, taking you toward filling the gaps in this life. The emptiness in your life is causing this sadness. Have patience; your emotional body is functioning. Give it time; it will change your feelings. When it does, you will achieve a balance between your heart and mind. Confidence will be the result of this.

"This is my advice: When you love somebody, and they reject it, don't keep giving love. If you have an excess of love to give, love them on a higher level; this includes a lover, friends, and children—all you give love to. This is the time to exercise unconditional love; it's called 'standing still' and allowing life to rearrange itself. Don't use unconditional love as an excuse to tolerate the inadequacies of others. Know the inadequacy is where a lesson lies; stand back and allow others to work through their difficulties. This is the right attitude to open the door to your future. It will prevent negative thoughts from entering your life because negative thoughts do harm. In fact, any form of criticism stops the soul from loving because love will never be coerced into the mind's viewpoint of how it should flow. Your love can become a river if you learn to stand back. Give people time to work through their difficulties. You are not in a race. When the river of love stops flowing, disease begins.

"Stand still at these times; train yourself to love others by letting them go. Not only will you keep your astral body clear, but those who truly love you will feel encouraged to take the plunge. The river of love has enough love for everyone. You have dived into the waters of soul love;

you are trying to swim back against the current because you are lonely. You are no longer the same person; part of you is illumined. Some of the cells in your body have been energised and spiritualised. You are more sensitive now. Don't feel you are lesser or weaker because you have lost the shell of defence that you created to protect your heart. Your soul can protect itself with its own love. Your increased sensitivity is your psychic powers reborn. Your psychic can now give you clear feelings, words, or pictures to help you understand where you are and where you are going, especially when you have a decision to make. Every time you drop down, close your eyes and ask your psychic to show you a picture to explain what's happening.

"What people fail to recognise is that destiny contains energy, and when this energy is felt it gives meaning to life, it gives purpose, but most of all it gives love. You can't find love by looking. You won't find destiny by wanting. They are found through living. I am asking you to let go unconditionally so that you can start living again. Do this for a time; when destiny finds you worthy of release, your life will change at such a speed that people you love will have no option but to look at their own lives. You do not realise the impact you have on those who love you. Your communication with spirit is so interesting to them that they look at your life instead of confronting themselves. When you help yourself, you will be helping them."

As I finished writing these words, I had to lie down to digest it all. Unconditional love seemed to be the key to remaining on one's destiny; loving in the right way was part of this.

Lovingly, Lalesha whispered, "Gently stand still. Wait for life to move over everything, including your finances. Have faith in life—God created it."

My mother used to say, "Man proposes: God disposes." These words used to make me angry. It was as if God had the right to change anything we put effort into. We would be stripped of any power; we were puppets. My experience with spirit guides was giving me power; proving that we no longer needed to be puppets. Lalesha was certainly not a puppet. Her powerful knowledge was freeing me from limitations. Everything she was teaching me had to be lived. In a way, she was teaching me to teach myself.

Her part of God was stimulating my part of God. Someone else's part of God was smiling as I went to sleep.

Chapter 25

Working with My Aura

For weeks, I consciously worked hard at loving myself through acknowledging destiny. When others came into my mind, I would try to love them unconditionally. Keeping an eye on my thoughts was extremely difficult. I became acutely aware that I truly had allowed my thoughts to run riot all over the place—from comparing my life with other people's to continuing to love people when they were not reciprocating.

All of this created confusion and prevented me from seeing my future clearly. If this confusion came back, I would read the affirmation Lalesha had given me. I would ask my higher self to align my thoughts with my soul's true destiny. Immediately, a confidence would envelop me, and the confusion would depart. This day, as I sat down to write out my shopping list before going to the supermarket, I decided to check my feelings, like Lalesha had said, by closing my eyes and allowing my psychic to show me a picture explaining where I was at. I could see myself surrounded in a mist, but this didn't disturb me. I had started to accept the journey instead of wanting to get to the destination. As I started to write down the items, Lalesha overlapped my thinking, blending with my shopping list. I was becoming used to her personal touch. Her interaction with the simple things to do with physical living was showing me everything could become spiritualised. I started writing down her words:

"Your auric field is a combination of all your bodies, your many selves. As you change, so does your aura. You could refer to it as your own weather map. The aura is what affects your physical health; the health of your body is the result of not only the food you eat but also the thoughts and feelings you have as you live life. If your past is moving out, a lot of white light will be present in your aura. When you are flowing and on your destiny, it will feel warm, looking like a glowing sun. When you are living through emotional sadness, it will look as if it is pouring rain. You are plotting your weather map with your thoughts and feelings. You are learning to control this through awareness—instead of being a victim to what you have created at the times you were unclear.

"Your past has started moving out of your aura—this is why it is misty. Things you regret or are ashamed of will not be removed unless you view them with understanding. Clearly look at what you have lived through—with unconditional love—and you will see the reason why you had to live through some of your past. If it ended in suffering, a lesson was present somewhere. Life is meant to make sense. If there was no reason, suffering would be senseless. When you find the reason, you can dismantle the block. Your auric field is your senses being exposed. This is what we see when we are called upon to help. The aura is what we work with. You are the owner of this energy; keep looking at your thoughts and continue to give your feelings consideration. When you observe yourself without blame, you clear away any misunderstandings or negativity. You promote your well-being by attracting genuine thoughts of love. This is how you clear the last fragments of your past. Continue with the process."

I felt quite warm when she left. Finishing my grocery list, I drove to the supermarket. I usually moved fast through the supermarket, always in a hurry to remove myself from the congestion of so many people. Today I went slowly, not even noticing the other people. Then, as I reached for my favourite coffee suddenly my past overwhelmed me. I had shopped at this supermarket throughout three broken relationships. I felt alone, single, and sad. No love was circulating in my aura, and my feelings were crying—not my eyes. Recalling what Lalesha had been teaching me, I forced myself to feel love by acknowledging I had a destiny. The past became more painful until it reached a point where I was numb. Using effort, I kept generating love for my future. It worked—love started returning to me. I could feel it flowing in my aura—and I wasn't trying to love anymore! I moved quickly through the rest of my shopping. I wanted to get home and find out from Lalesha what was occurring.

When I arrived home, the love continued flowing. My suffering was also surfacing—without any pain. In fact, I loved my suffering. Leaving the groceries in the car, I rushed inside and picked up my pen. Lalesha was right there.

"When a person goes through hurt, the electrical circuits in the brain that generate love short-circuit and are damaged. Because you made an effort to love, this ignited the circuits, connecting you to your own soul centre. You can compare this to exercising at the gym. As you put effort into an exercise that is painful, your body reaches a point—through effort—that releases its own endorphins, moving you onto a high. It is the same with your mind; through effort, you can attain a release. You are now being replenished. This is the perfect time to reflect upon your past. I will leave you as you do this. Remember, when the love stops flowing, start loving again."

The love was flowing as I walked back to the car to rescue my groceries. At the end of the day, I sat in the kitchen and reflected on my past experiences with love. Suffering was still present, but there was no pain. I realised I didn't want to let the suffering go; it had become an excuse—something I could lean upon in my lonely times. It was more the real me than the 'me' others had known. This suffering had initiated my journey toward knowing spirit; it had been my greatest friend. I didn't really want to let it go, but if I was going to be free to love again, this self-pity would have to go. I could feel love standing by me as if it was waiting for my feelings to catch up.

Although I hadn't physically done much all day, I was so tired. Lalesha had explained how the physical body gained its energy from the aura as well as from food. I'd eaten enough healthy food that it had to be my aura. After all the feelings I had experienced, it was understandable that it needed replenishing. I went to bed, hoping my out-of-body experiences would do this. I also wanted this activity to bring me up to date with where I was on my journey.

Chapter 26

Withdrawal Symptoms

As the weeks went by, I could feel my aura getting stronger. At times, I was disappointed by the effects that loving myself were producing. Friends I had loved throughout many difficult times were withdrawing from me. Lalesha had warned me about this, but it wasn't easy.

I visualised white light regularly; it helped me come to the conclusion that if they loved my old self and I was changing, a natural process of separation would have to occur. Otherwise, their love could prevent the new me from expressing. Even though this made sense, it didn't help my financial position. Many who were withdrawing were clients; despite what Lalesha had said, I decided to put my house on the market. I started to enthusiastically clean up for the eventual sale.

While going through old photos, I realised I couldn't feel my past. It was weird: the suffering was gone, but a new suffering was presenting itself. This suffering was called detachment. I felt disconnected to everything around me. I couldn't stop the process; I knew I had reached a place of no-return. The only option was to keep moving forward. I was getting sick of loving myself; it felt so selfish not to give. I asked Lalesha about the growing dislike of loving myself. She laughed. Surprised, I questioned her light-heartedness over my situation.

"Dear one, you are going through withdrawal symptoms from your past attachments. This is what occurs when one moves from one level to another. Attachments are not wrong, but you have changed your level of love—and new attachments will occur in your future. This is the in-between time; keep believing in your future or you will lose the level you are attaining. You know you can't go backwards because your love of the past isn't strong enough to hold you there anymore. You can't go forward because destiny hasn't arrived yet. This is an important part of your journey. The instability involved as one goes through this level of detachment causes many to question the stability of their minds. The function of withdrawal symptoms is to transmute the past. One cannot let go of the past without experiencing withdrawal symptoms; it is the same with unconditional love. One cannot love unconditionally without accepting the level the other person is on. Letting go cannot occur without these feelings playing their parts in the process. If psychiatrists and counsellors looked for the lesson in the mindsets their patients were stuck with—and encouraged them to face these lessons as well as finding a focus for their future—moving a person to the next step would be easier.

"You are going through a process of alignment. A medical doctor assessing your state-of-mind would put you on antidepressants, but you would never get to flow with your destiny because drugs create separation. Depression is a natural sign that one is not flowing toward destiny. All people go through different states of mind. Most people are too scared to acknowledge they are in this state—let alone mention it to a doctor or friend. Fear is the biggest block for humanity to overcome. It can help to know the soul keeps moving. It won't stop. It was designed this way; it doesn't need physical rest like your body does. It is always working around what the human being does in the hope of making contact. If the human mind ignores these impulses from the soul, it withdraws. If you keep loving your soul, you will keep it close. Sharing with others is what you are missing; your soul was designed to integrate all levels of life. Don't worry. Just a little bit longer and the withdrawal symptoms will have transmuted the last bit of energy that is blocking your new cycle from manifesting. You will socialise with others again. Love the suffering involved in non-attachment. Love the withdrawal symptoms; they are helping you be free."

Once again, Lalesha had made sense by reassuring me that I only had to go through a short process. Even though I didn't enjoy being so detached, it was removing my past suffering. I embraced the last pangs of withdrawal symptoms. I knew by going within—through treating my thoughts and feelings as real—was aligning me with my soul. This was important. Lalesha had explained how the soul held the power; when it made the decision to withdraw, we had to follow. Nannette had found this out during her transition to the Other Side. I went to sleep, hoping to meet my soul outside of my body to see how in agreement I was with my destiny.

Chapter 27

The Staircase to My Soul

Time continued moving; as it did, I noticed the withdrawal symptoms were being replaced with more love. I could feel it circulating in my aura. Since I could also feel love for my house, I decided to weather the financial storm and stay put. The only disturbing influence was I had woken up with Cliff on my mind, and I still hadn't heard from him. I didn't expect to, but in my mind he was 'there'. I couldn't decide whether this was brought about by letting him go unconditionally or whether the opportunity was still there for him to be in my future. I decided to let go and bring myself down to the earth plane with the physical exercise of everyday living. This was no good. I still couldn't get him out of my mind, so I went off to the gym.

Back on the rower again, I closed my eyes to take a look. There he was, surrounded in warm gold light. This time, I pulled my feelings back and focused them into loving myself. It worked! The picture of him disappeared. However, while doing stomach crunches, I rubbed my itchy ear. I felt as if I was rubbing his ear. I could clearly feel his face. This was fascinating. It wasn't disturbing, but it did make me think of him more. I exercised until these thoughts left, happy to arrive in the sauna and relax.

No one else was present. Lying on my stomach in the dry heat, I started seeing gold light flowing from my tailbone to the top of my head. As I observed the gold light moving, other colours started to generate around my body. Healing was occurring. I could feel it moving throughout my body like a thousand laser lights. Then a male spirit guide in creamy gold robes entered my auric atmosphere. I felt I knew his presence, but I still asked him who he was.

"I am Larsha, Lalesha's male counterpart. Whilst she is away gathering your future together, I am here for your final understanding."

I rushed out of the sauna and grabbed my pen and paper. As he telepathically spoke, the colours around me increased in size.

"Larsha, what am I seeing?"

"You are experiencing your heavenly soul, the light from your eternal flame, your spirit that existed before you experienced this earth's consciousness. You have travelled home, mentally in consciousness, through your efforts to untangle many thoughts that all have a connection with a past life experience. Through contact with the heavenly soul, a person can access spirit's energy and become unlimited. The gold light moving up your spine was called the kundalini by ancient masters on this planet. When you contact your heavenly soul, you stimulate your own kundalini into action, and vice versa. The colours generated each have a different frequency, and all work toward healing and regenerating the body. You can help this process by visually focusing on each colour. Start with the colours of a rainbow, and move each colour from the base of your spine to the top of your head. Begin with the colour red."

This guide was slightly different from Lalesha. His asking was like a command. I went back into the sauna and lay down to practise what he was saying. As I started visualising the colours, I saw my spine as a framework. As each colour moved from the base of my spine to my skull, I could see, feel, and hear my back being aligned. I looked at my physical flesh for changes—it would be nice if a few wrinkles could go!

"Stop! You are putting more emphasis on the body; vanity is a distraction from the light. Stay with the kundalini; it stimulates healing throughout the system without physical interference. Look at the scintillating colours; your body will naturally try to meet up to the vibration from each colour if you don't think about what your body looks like. Hold control by staying focused on light; it is real, and your body will respond to this over time. Eventually your body will become accustomed to following the light. Your sexuality has moved from the level of—"

I shot out of my kundalini—male spirit guide or not. "Does this mean I will never experience sex again?"

He didn't laugh like Lalesha, but he smiled.

"Purity of the senses makes way for heightened feeling, not the diminishing of feeling. Your body has been used to living off your emotions, leaving you exhausted. Emotions are meant to ebb and flow like the tide; however, you are not just your emotions. You began with a heavenly soul that has the ability to release enough energy to keep you moving, especially at times like this when you do not have a mate. Raising your kundalini will free your body from the craving for this man you feel you love."

So, I still hadn't let go of him! Amazing. Maybe he was the male part of my heavenly soul! This spirit guide knew something.

"When I was exercising today, I could feel Cliff's body. In fact, I felt I was him. Can you help me understand this please?"

"You have overlapped with his energy because he is one of your original soul mates, like Lalesha said. You can't stop feeling love for him, but you can discipline your love by loving him unconditionally. You have been doing this, but when you felt his presence this morning, you let go of loving him unconditionally as you became caught up with what you were seeing. Continue to practise letting go again so you won't interfere with his pathway—or yours. It's your future we are concerned with. If the need for a man in your life is necessary, we will help it happen.

"Are you asking me to open the door for another man?"

"Be careful."

"Why?" I suddenly felt very confident with the lighted activity around me.

Looking quite serious, he said, "When one obtains a flow from the heavenly soul, the mind becomes more powerful—and the aura becomes magnetic. This is when love must be expressed 'purely'. If you share with another man who is not your chosen soul mate, you will lose this flow from your heavenly soul and drop to the level of the personality of the one you are sharing with. You will have to work your way up to freedom again. You have been earning this freedom to have a connection with your heavenly soul. The synchronicity of your life won't take place until every level is completed. In the meantime, your heavenly soul—if you remain connected—will protect you from making a mistake and creating another scene in this play of your life.

"You need this time to exercise freedom on your own. Become accustomed to the beauty of naturally flowing with light. You are now ready to view part of your blueprint. Tonight your old friend Nannette will visit you in your consciousness. I must go now. Take no thought. Breathe."

And in one breath, he was gone. I started to feel where I was on my journey; with this new freedom, I could be myself. Confidence was emerging. I put away my pen and paper and headed for the shower, reflecting on Nannette's presence when she last travelled to me. She was happy working as a guide; it would be interesting to communicate with her again. Her experiences on the Other Side were different from what I was going through, although the same message of love was present. I started to become enthusiastic over what Larsha had said; he called Nannette my old friend. She was a friend who had made it home complete.

As I thought of this, Nannette arrived; she shone a light, like a torch, on me. "I will wait until your excitement dies down, and then I'll come back."

I was excited; news from Nannette about my future was what I needed to hear. Larsha had said I was ready to view part of my blueprint. This I wanted to see, so I lived through the rest of the day preparing my mind by focusing on lovely, clear white light.

Evening came. The children were asleep. The night was still after a very windy day. I sat ready with my pen. Nannette arrived.

"Have you chosen yet, dear?"

"Chosen what?"

"What window you wish to view your blueprint from."

This took me by surprise. "I thought it was just a level or state of heightened perception that enables one to view their blueprint."

"There are many mansions on the Other Side, and they all relate to how one thinks and feels. The state of heightened perception is the doorway. The view from the windows is created from your feelings (how you have loved). Each window relates to a level and will give you a different perspective over the landscape of your life."

"Is there an attic?" I asked, wanting to see the whole picture.

"Yes, there is an attic. A stairway leads to this room. It is long, and every step is a lifetime."

I hesitated, knowing I would view the scene easily when it was time to pass over. "Is there a window from which I can view this life I am living now?"

"Yes. It is in the attic. You must still walk up the stairs."

Feeling courageous, I decided part of the way wasn't good enough. I had come this far; I wanted to see it all.

"Take me to the attic," I said.

She took my hand, and we started moving. My body remained writing it all down, but I was moving in my consciousness, and it felt real.

As we walked on each step, Nannette would wait, asking me what I could sense. On the first step, all I could feel was powerful, clear colours moving through me—similar to how Larsha had described my heavenly soul. Then I felt enormous love in my heart.

"That was your first incarnation. The way you looked and were has now been transmuted. Love is a signal that the essence of that experience has returned to you. Much healing was expressed in that lifetime. An ability to heal is within you; it's your choice if you wish to use it. You don't have to because you have lived many lives healing people."

Step by step, she helped me to absorb many previous lifetimes of experience. My heart was overflowing with love as I felt the essence from each lifetime. When we were closer to the top, I stood on a step that felt transcendent. I thought I was 'there'.

"Is this the last step?" I asked.

"This is another past life. It was a life in Egypt where you had everything—love, power, ascendancy. Toward the end of this incarnation, you used your power unwisely. That is why the last step, the one we are heading toward, is the hardest."

"If I had everything I wanted, where did I go wrong?"

"You loved possessively. Your love of perfection, coupled with your perception of God at that time in history, made you try to obtain eternal life on earth in that one physical incarnation. You surrounded yourself with beauty and love. Earth became heaven, and you would not allow any family member to move out of this circle of perfection. You limited their experiences by doing this. You have worked through most of this; the residue left within your subconscious mind can be cleared in a simple way by having the attitude that if a loved one makes a decision that you know will cause them suffering, you must not consider it to be a wrong decision. You must delight in the truth that all decisions are based on the level of love a person needs to experience. The clear soul you see in those you love is there for each individual to discover. All must drink from their own well; it is their personal journey. You are attaining yours right now. You will know what I mean when you finish the last chapter. A few more steps to go, then we will be at the top."

We reached the last step. It didn't feel that stable.

"What's the matter?" she said.

"Well, if this is the last step, and it's my present life, it doesn't feel as good as my past lives."

"You haven't finished this life yet. Love comes in full at the beginning of a lifetime and returns at the ending. During all the in-between times, one must work hard giving of this love. You can compare it to a relationship."

"Nannette, I have just been through a process of loving myself. I haven't been giving love to anybody, yet you are saying life is for giving love and reminding me of partnerships. I believe this. I don't enjoy the selfishness of loving myself."

"Don't be so hard on yourself, dear. After this experience, you will return with much love to give. All people must get to the place of loving themselves when they are finishing an old cycle. It's the same as dying. When one passes over, the first step is self-examination—and then love of self before the future can be viewed. You are bored of loving yourself, yet you are scared to start sharing love again. Even though you have cleared away the painful past, you haven't had enough time to heal. This is why you cannot move from the position of loving yourself yet. The view of your blueprint will help you to trust. Do you have any questions before we look?"

"Yes. Will this be my last life on earth?"

"If you attain freedom to love, yes. Fulfilment of this lifetime is important. The blueprint of your new cycle remains here. How do you feel?"

"Too tired to take a look!"

"Well, you won't lose that tiredness unless you look. So here we go—the view from the attic!"

This was a shock. As we stood on the step, it transformed itself into a room with windows and blinds that were pulled down. Very little light was in the room, and it was filled with pictures of people. Piles of pictures were stacked against the wall; others were hanging on the wall—even the ceiling was covered. Cobwebs draped the entire room, but they were white, like lace. I couldn't see myself anywhere.

"If this is my last life, then who are all the people in these pictures? Are they my past lives?"

"These are your attachments—souls you have loved before."

"If this is my stairway to my soul, how did they get here? Are they ghosts?"

"Are you a ghost? No, you are not. Your body is still functioning writing this down whilst part of you is here in this room with me. You are at a level in your life where you are meeting up and letting go of all soul mates you have loved. As you do this, the pictures will depart. One will remain. This one has the right to share your soul and be here with you."

"Do I have to study each picture and then let go? I thought I had cleared my life up. I have been asking to be free of attachments, trying so hard to stand alone."

"You have been moving; you are not resting on your soul. However, there are a few details left to tidy up your life for the future. You need a greater soul connection for this flow."

My thoughts quickly caught on to what she was really saying. In a nice way, she was hinting that I needed to dedicate myself more fully to working with spirit guides to fulfil my chosen destiny. As soon as I accepted this challenge, with help from the heightened energy circulating around me, I released myself into the feeling. It was like diving into the ocean of consciousness; and as I did this the blinds went up, and I was staring at a starry night sky, pulsating with activity.

"Look! This is your soul's consciousness; you have opened the door through your commitment to spirit. Now all your attachments will connect with their own souls. Soon your room will almost be empty. You can now go to sleep down on your earthly bed. Many clearings will now happen as much work has been achieved. Part of you will remain here with me, viewing your personal blueprint amongst your soul group. In the morning, you will be given inspiration to start living it."

"Why can't I see the blueprint now?"

"You are viewing the entire blueprint of your living soul. It is your earthly life that you wish to see. This will be given to you in pieces. As you complete living each piece, another shall be given. Tomorrow I will place the first piece of the picture in your aura. When it has synchronised and become part of your earthly life, another piece shall be given. These pieces are all part of the new structure about to form itself as a new cycle in this life. The synergy required to absorb these pieces needs your love. You have tried so hard on your own that you have lost faith in your future. Arms of love carried you into your first life; that love surrounds you now. Trust. After the first few pieces have been lived through, your life will start to change; the piece you have been waiting for—to feel complete—will arrive later. That is when you will start a new adventure, and you will not be alone. Love is starting to surround you. Give your heartfelt expectations of love full reign, and you will travel to the heart of your consciousness. You are there now, yet you are still awake, writing this. Go to sleep, and the last fragments of the old you will be absorbed into this almighty consciousness that can be termed *soul love*."

I followed her guidance, knowing she was a trusted soul friend. The trauma I would awaken to the next day was impossible to envisage because pure, pulsating love was encapsulating my mind, drawing me into a very deep sleep.

Chapter 28

Closure

When I awoke, the view Nannette had shown me was still resident in my mind, but my decision to follow my heart as I drifted off to sleep didn't feel so good. In fact, it felt like the last step, unstable, and I was feeling shaky. Consoling myself that this nervousness was the result of experiencing a higher vibration in contrast to my human life, I made myself get out of bed to drink a glass of water. The glass hit the top of the tap, shattering it into tiny pieces. As I observed the glass breaking, I became the glass. This was exactly how I felt:

What an unusual day!

I looked outside—it was pouring rain.

The phone rang—it was Cliff.

No excitement was present within me.

I couldn't even recognise his voice—it sounded distant.

I tried hard to focus on what he was saying,

"I'm sorry; I've met someone else who lives in the same city where I live."

"It's more convenient."

"I'm sorry."

If convenience was a word I was used to living by, it would have made sense. A convenience reminded me of a toilet. My life, my work, my children—the whole spectrum of living—had never been convenient. Working in with others had always been difficult, but sharing those times was always worth the effort.

Now, at this point, I had become an inconvenience to Cliff; this was the ultimate knockback, especially since he was one of my original soul mates. I picked up the pieces of glass from the sink. As I wrapped the glass in yesterday's newspaper, feeling like yesterday, I tried to come to terms with the reality that—as far as Cliff was concerned—I was yesterday's news. Somewhere in my consciousness, there was a love for him I could not deny—and I did not want it there anymore. The spirit guides were not going to avoid explaining this scenario to me. I wanted to know—and now! I rushed through the housework. The toilet was overflowing. I tried to phone a plumber, but all were busy. I dropped the children off at school, missing the gym, and rushed back home, scared the toilet might overflow even more and leave sewage all over the floor.

I returned home to find my loving friend, Sue, on my doorstep. With tears of exhaustion from the stress of finally accepting the closure with Cliff, I sat down and told her of the morning's events. She was shocked at the news since she had her own mindset of how this relationship would end up. At this moment, the toilet was my main concern. It was connected to a septic tank and could lead to bigger problems, but we attempted to fix it together. Thankfully, it was only a small blockage, and we fixed it. Sue started laughing at this experience.

"What are you laughing for? I'm suffering!"

"Sorry. I can't help it; your life has turned to shit. Let's ask the guides."

Hesitantly I sat in front of a recording device; before I started, I remembered my psychic had been informing me for weeks that he had met someone else. I hadn't wanted to acknowledge this—I was too busy writing—and I ignored it with the hope that he would be there at the end of the book. This was a shock to my expectation of him—not to my inner knowing. Lalesha started by advising me to move into my heavenly soul.

"Your human self is going through a cleansing, but your heavenly soul doesn't need to. This situation requires a bit more than unconditional love; you need a healing from us. Visualise a silver triangle above your head filled with mauve light. When you see, feel, and almost taste this light, it will be working, protecting your heart from undeserved pain."

I mentally questioned why I needed protection. I didn't think he wanted to cause me any suffering.

"No, he does not, but his life at present is harming you. Inwardly, he knows this. Remember the astral body—the body of thought I spoke to you about?"

"Yes."

"Well, because both of you were linked on an astral level, your astral bodies must now go through a process of unravelling as separation takes place on this level. This could only take weeks—not months—but when it happens, you won't think of him anymore. The more you visualise the triangle, the quicker it will occur. Try not to be hurt; you know this is the level of love he needs to progress as a soul. You are finally learning non-possessive love. However painful it is at present, you will look back at this time as one of your greatest accomplishments. Practising unconditional love will serve you well in the future; you will be able to stand back when many of your loved ones make decisions that cause them suffering. You will remember that decisions are based on a level of love, and levels of love are formed for the sake of learning. Unconditional love gives others space to grow; however hard it seems, in the future, you will do this with a smile on your face. If you could laugh at your present predicament, your pain would be over. You can't! Not from lack of trying, but because your emotions need time to adjust. Constantly share your love with your heavenly soul and you will be prepared for whatever happens in your life. You can do this by doing what Larsha told you. Gently visualise each colour of the rainbow moving from the base of your spine to the top of your head. This will keep you balanced. Don't forget to also visualise the silver triangle at the times you feel pain. He is going to feel your final withdrawal; there has been a karmic configuration. This was unavoidable; it is related to your Egyptian life that Nannette spoke of as a step. Your slate is now clear. Keep it that way by staying within the mauve light at the times you feel sensitive. This will protect you from resorting to resentment, bitterness, and the weakness to never love again. I will return when you are ready to begin your new cycle."

With the kind help from my friend cooking tea and seeing to the children, I went to bed early contemplating all the different levels of love I had experienced.

I knew the visualisation of this silver triangle was protecting my love at this time, so I placed my love inside the triangle, where it was safe. Powerful, intense love entered my head from outside of myself. I could not identify this love as any person I had known. I knew this was non-possessive love, and I wanted it more than I wanted him. My level of love was about to change direction. As a sensitive Cancerian, I yearned for the ability to laugh at the dramas in life. Viewed from the triangle, life truly looked like a play. Feeling very protected, I went to sleep with the knowledge that this type of suffering could be gracefully overcome by working with spirit guides.

Chapter 29

Freedom to Love

On Sunday morning, I felt positive. White light was moving through my mind, and there were no dark shadows. I pulled the curtains back, and the warm sun streamed onto my bed. It was the first day of summer, December in New Zealand. I decided to walk across the road to dive into the ocean. The water was cold but invigorating. As I walked back to have a shower and eat breakfast, I contemplated how young I was feeling. Part of me didn't want to ever leave this house. Living so near the beach was healing me.

"Wrong! Your soul is healing you, giving you youth—not the physical plane."

It was Larsha! I picked up my pen.

"During the night, you travelled with Lalesha to the soul plane, and you reviewed your past. You saw how your original bubble of joy, your heavenly soul, had become distanced from your consciousness. Out of the body, your soul took control, putting what you no longer wanted from your past in one pile and what you did want in another. You then transferred your attention into the future; the past has been lived through. There are no lessons left from your past; this is why you feel so good."

"What does this mean to my human life?"

"You have a new cycle to live through. You have two choices for how this cycle can manifest. One is to sell your home and relocate to another city; following this direction would eventuate in you working as a medium with a soul partner by your side. You would fulfil a happy life if you took this road. The other choice, which both Lalesha and I hope you will consider, is remaining in this home and continuing to write. Lalesha has a lot of information that she wants you to bring through. It will be very demanding, and you won't be able to have a mate by your side whilst you do this because bringing through this guidance will require all your energy. If you choose to dedicate yourself to this purpose, the reward will be great."

"But if I don't sell my house, how can I exist financially?"

"Yes, your past has left you with difficulties on the human plane. Your soul wishes you to write a list of these difficulties. When you have done this, put the list beside your bed. Each night as you go off to sleep, ask the Benevolent Beings of Light to find a solution to each problem. Every morning when you wake up, sense the guidance from your nightly excursions. Look for signs of relief as you live through the day. Follow your intuition; you may be given something to say or do. As you act upon this, you will be amazed at the solutions that come.

"Write the list and include everything—right down to health problems. If energy can create an illness, then energy can create a cure. There is an antidote for everything; for example, when one is on the road of destiny, it boosts the immune system. Once your new destiny is flowing, you will be amazed at your good health. You are moving into a cycle where proof becomes the way-shower. Interestingly enough, you will become the proof of our teachings."

"That's an enormous responsibility. I can't be perfect."

"Your imperfections are becoming transmuted. You like the feeling, don't you?"

"Yes, but others may criticise me from their levels. Investigating my many knockbacks has brought me to this level of love, but others don't know this. They look at my outer life—not my inner experience. I have been judged many times in my life."

"Judging is the old way. Who can cast the first stone? Those who cannot face themselves are in this category. You have taken responsibility on many levels; it always takes time for one's human life to catch up to soul achievements. In the meantime, equilibrium between your heavenly soul and the human you is happening. When this process is complete, you will be immune to negative thoughts. You will only attract what is beneficial to your life.

"This is the difference between positive thinking and soul awareness. Of course soul responds to positive thinking, but sometimes positive thinking can cut out the beautiful flows from the soul via one's intuition. Positive thinking can be a crutch to avoid facing a truth; this is when soul can be ignored. Righteousness has never worked on this planet—and it never will. If you love the trial and error of your own efforts, the times you feel positive will be real—and not enforced by mind control. To control the mind is to stop the soul from having input. If you will something to occur solely for yourself, then you are also enforcing your will upon others because life is about people. This dominance will not be allowed anymore. It is why the monetary system is failing. Giving and sharing with gentleness creates a power that is eternal.

"Every loving action you make will have a beneficial reaction on somebody because love naturally flows when you give to others. All people have goodness inside; it is their heavenly soul. If it's not present, it's awaiting the right time. All souls have a time to wake up. This is your time of renewal; until you make a decision about which road you wish to take, you need to remain independent. When one is independent, they are only relating to themselves. This is a protection from interference and is being enforced with you at this time. If you listened to friends, you would share their will—and then you would not be able to have the freedom to follow your own soul."

"What if I become so used to following my own soul that I never wish to confine myself to another's will, including a partner?"

"You will not have to. When your heavenly soul has been absorbed by your human self, and you are strongly stable, only a person that can harmonise fully will connect with you."

"Thank you, Larsha. This finally makes sense."

"Your efforts will result in pure positive energy. If you act on this, your life will start moving rapidly. Forget what others think. Start writing your list. When you go to sleep tonight, dream of a Day of Love for Everyone; all of humanity will eventually get there. I'm off now to help another of humanity."

"Larsha, you are so wise. Are you a heavenly soul?"

"Yes, I am."

"I wish you were in a physical body."

"I am."

"What? I thought I was talking to a spirit guide."

"You are."

"Where is your human body?"

"Going through lessons—like you."

I was stunned. He was helping me from his heavenly soul. *Was it possible that I could meet his human self?* I started to sense the darkness of my past in contrast to the future. He turned and looked back at me:

Ask and you will receive.
When the wings of love move, aim high,
Focus toward a destination
And when it has been reached, aim for another.
Never stop loving and your journey will last forever.
You have attained freedom to love.

Epilogue

What an unusual ending. It was not the one I'd expected, but while working with spirit guides, I have learned that you constantly adapt. I've noticed this is always compensated by the constant reassurance that you will reach your goals. It truly is a never-ending journey when you share your life with spirit guides. There is never a dull moment.

Nannette, Larsha, and Lalesha were setting the stage for a clearer future for me. I had to work hard toward attaining this. The steps along the way are when we move forward and grow up—or stop still and grow old. Too often we wait for life to change our lives, yet the key lies within.

I waited a few weeks after I'd finished writing, and recalling what Larsha had said about my two pathways—I sat and meditated. A happy relationship was very inviting. Working with spirit guides to gain information that would help people, was also appealing. The guides had helped me through so many difficult times that I wanted to give something back. Every time I imagined following this pathway, my heart would jump with enthusiasm. That is the direction I chose. Little did I know the information from Lalesha would take ten years to bring through.

This next book is almost completed. The same message of love is present, but it expands with information on how to integrate with our multidimensional self (our many bodies), and this is what the new Aquarian Age requires. It is called *Another Dimension of Love.*

About the Author

Gina Ravenswood, a mother of five children, has worked as a medium for more than thirty years. She lives in New Zealand. She writes, does readings, and takes development groups in a quiet village by the sea. Her main love is helping people gain their own guidance and fulfil their destinities.